Gary M. Lawson

Ida A. Green.
Nov. 1911.
Y. W. C. A.
14 + Castro
Oakland
Cal.

GOD'S MESSAGE TO
THE HUMAN SOUL

THE COLE LECTURES

1907
God's Message to the Human Soul
By John Watson (Ian Maclaren). *The Cole Lectures, prepared, but not delivered.* Cloth, - net 1.25.

1906
Christ and Science
Jesus Christ regarded as the Center of Science. By Francis Henry Smith, University of Virginia. Cloth, - - - net 1.25.

1905
The Universal Elements of the Christian Religion
An attempt to Interpret Contemporary Religious Conditions. By Charles Cuthbert Hall, President Union Theological Seminary, New York. Cloth, - - net 1.25.

1903
The Religion of the Incarnation
By Eugene Russell Hendrix. One of the Bishops of the M. E. Church, South. Cloth, - - net 1.00.

*The Cole Lectures of Vanderbilt
University for 1907*

God's Message to the Human Soul

The Use of the Bible in the
Light of the New Knowledge

By
JOHN WATSON, D.D.
(*Ian Maclaren*)

NEW YORK   CHICAGO   TORONTO
Fleming H. Revell Company
LONDON   AND   EDINBURGH

Copyright, 1907, by
FLEMING H. REVELL COMPANY

SECOND EDITION

New York: 158 Fifth Avenue
Chicago: 80 Wabash Avenue
Toronto: 25 Richmond Street, W.
London: 21 Paternoster Square
Edinburgh: 100 Princes Street

THE COLE LECTURES

THE late Colonel E. W. Cole of Nashville, Tennessee, donated to Vanderbilt University the sum of five thousand dollars, afterwards increased by Mrs. E. W. Cole to ten thousand, the design and conditions of which gift are stated as follows:

"The object of this fund is to establish a foundation for a perpetual Lectureship in connection with the Biblical Department of the University, to be restricted in its scope to a defense and advocacy of the Christian religion. The lectures shall be delivered at such intervals, from time to time, as shall be deemed best by the Board of Trust; and the particular theme and lecturer shall be determined by nomination of the Theological Faculty and confirmation of the College of Bishops of the Methodist Episcopal Church, South. Said lecture shall always be reduced to writing in full, and the manuscript of the same shall be the property of the University, to be published or disposed of by the Board of Trust at its discretion, the net proceeds arising therefrom to be added to the foundation fund, or otherwise used for the benefit of the Biblical Department."

In Memoriam

REV. JOHN WATSON, D. D., more popularly known throughout the world of letters by his nom de plume of Ian Maclaren, was born in Essex, England, November 3, 1850. Having been educated in Scotland and Germany, he was licensed to preach by the Free Church of Scotland in 1874, and after serving as pastor in Edinburgh, Logie-almond, and Glasgow, he became in 1880 pastor of the Sefton Park Presbyterian Church of Liverpool, England, which position he resigned in 1905, in order to devote his time more largely to authorship and the lecture field. He is the author of eighteen volumes, being best known by those titled " Beside the Bonnie Brier Bush," 1894 ; " The Days of Auld Lang Syne," 1895 ; " The Upper Room," 1895 ; " The Mind of the Master," 1896 ; " The Cure of Souls " (Lyman Beecher Lectures at Yale University), 1896 ; " A Doctor of the Old School," 1897 ; " The Doctrines of Grace,"

1900; "The Life of the Master," 1901; and "The Inspiration of Faith," 1905. To these must now be added "God's Message to the Human Soul," 1907.

In the spring of 1907 Dr. Watson came to America to deliver the Cole Lectures of Vanderbilt University, and to fill other engagements. On April 22d he was taken suddenly and seriously ill, while at Mount Pleasant, Iowa, and two weeks later, on May 6th, the entire American nation, to whom the name of Ian Maclaren had become a household word, was stricken with unspeakable grief at the announcement of his death.

Introduction

THIS volume contains Dr. Watson's last message to the world. That it should consist of his maturest thoughts concerning the Bible, viewed as God's message to the human soul, seems strangely providential, now that his lips have been silenced by death.

The contents of this volume were to have been delivered as the Cole Lectures of Vanderbilt University for 1907. The date fixed for their delivery was the week extending from April 28th to May 5th. On Monday, May 6th, Dr. Watson died without ever having reached the seat of the University. The lectures, however, had been carefully prepared with a view to immediate publication after their delivery, and the manuscript was therefore practically ready for the printer when the author died.

The fame of Dr. Watson as preacher,

lecturer, and author, has gone wherever the English language is known. Nor is it confined by any means to the English-speaking world. Combining, as he did in his personality, so much that was strongest and best in the English and Scotch character, it is not to be wondered at that he was a great favourite in America. Of all the Englishmen and Scotchmen who have visited the United States during recent years, no one has spoken to larger audiences or received more marked evidences of his personal popularity than has the author of this volume. The unexpected death of our distinguished visitor, under conditions so pathetic, thus far away from his home, brought grief and tears to many thousands of Americans, who, while perusing the pages of " Beside the Bonnie Brier Bush," " A Doctor of the Old School," and " Auld Lang Syne," had learned for the first time what it was to read a book with melted hearts and moistened eyes. But would any other than a pathetic death have been a fit ending to the life of one whose greatest power was that of pathos, and whose pathos had been most powerful when describing scenes of death, whether of the lowly cottager among the heath-covered hills of Scotland, or of the Great Sufferer who died on the Cross of Calvary?

It is rarely given to any man to be great in more than one line of intellectual activity. Dr. Watson, however, stood not only *facile princeps* as a writer of stories of incomparable tenderness and beauty, but he was also great as a preacher and lecturer, and as a scholar and author. He preached to crowded houses in the Sefton Park Presbyterian Church in Liverpool, of which he was pastor from 1880 to 1905, and he was never more popular than when he closed his ministry there, at the end of twenty-five years of uninterrupted service. As a lecturer in institutions of learning and on the public platform, he had few equals. His gifts of conversation and anecdote made him the admired centre in every social circle which he adorned with his presence. Some of his published stories are among the immortelles of English literature; they are the creations of a genius that was rarely gifted in the power to turn life's prose into poetry and to idealize and immortalize places and characters and scenes which to many were only homely and commonplace things.

His contributions to religious and theological literature are of a high order. They represent sound scholarship and the best type of evangelical faith. Only when compared, and because compared, with his own matchless stories and idealizations, can they suffer any discount. They are volumes that dispel doubt and minister to faith, while they nourish at once both the intellectual and the spiritual man. The paths that he travelled were not the sidetracks and bypaths, but the great highways of thought and study in the realm of Biblical and theological literature.

The present volume, "God's Message to the Human Soul—The Use of the Bible in the Light of the New Knowledge," is one of the best that ever came from his pen. The different chapters were written especially with a view to meeting the needs of young ministers in our day. The author's thought is that the best result that comes from the new study and new knowledge of the Bible is the light it throws, and the emphasis it places, upon the Holy Scriptures as God's message to the human soul. Whatever interpretation of the Bible will impart to it this highest ethical value is the interpretation which the author accounts the truest and best, and this regardless of whether it is called "traditional theology" or "higher criticism." Into the discussion of purely critical questions pertaining to the Bible he does not enter, but some of the results of the modern scholar's method of studying the Bible he does assume as true because they seem to him to furnish the best foundation for interpreting the Bible as God's message of moral truth to the human soul. Theologians of all evangelical types of faith and of all schools of thought can well afford to allow to each other large liberty of opinion in the many minor points of Biblical interpretation if they will all only endeavour so to interpret and teach and preach the Bible as to give it the greatest possible power in leading men to give up sin, to be pure in mind and holy in heart, and to find an altruistic service and sacrifice for others the true ideal of the Christian life. If the minister in his study so interprets the Holy Scriptures, then these scriptures will always be, as expounded by him, a living message of God to the souls of men.

If the reader shall find some sentences in this volume which he thinks open to criticism, it is well that he should remind himself of the fact that these lectures are being published without having been delivered and without the author having had an opportunity to give the manuscript a careful and final reading. In editing the lectures for publication the writer has not felt that it was proper for him to make any alterations in the manuscript, even though he would have suggested that this be done in at least a few instances had the author lived to deliver the lectures and to personally supervise their publication.

The Cole Lectureship of Vanderbilt University is to be congratulated in that it was permitted to call forth from this gifted preacher and author before he died a message of such absorbing interest and lasting value to the Christian world as that which is contained in this volume.

       WILBUR F. TILLETT.

Dean's Office,
 Biblical Department,
  Vanderbilt University.
September 2, 1907.

Contents

THE CONSTRUCTION OF THE BOOK	. 19
THE STANDPOINT OF THE BOOK	. 61
THE HUMANITY OF THE BOOK	. 103
THE AUTHORITY OF THE BOOK	. 145
THE STYLE OF THE BOOK	. 189
THE USE OF THE BOOK	. 229

LECTURE I
THE CONSTRUCTION OF THE BOOK

LECTURE I

THE CONSTRUCTION OF THE BOOK

AS the Bible is the manual of the Christian minister, the instrument with which he is to do his work, it is in the last degree desirable that he should have an easy mastery of the Book. If it be his sword for smiting sin, he must know how to wield it, so that his strokes may not fall upon empty air, but may be deadly in conviction. If it be his vial of oil for healing sorrow, he must have a deft hand for applying the salve to the wound, so as to restore health. Within the compass of this extended and varied literature, there are resources of light and love for all ages, and all conditions, but the preacher must know how to find them, and when to use them. He must know how to make the correspondence between this eternal Book and every age, between this universal Book and every individual, and therefore the efficient minister has transferred the book from his table into his mind and into his heart. It is a benefit that he be trained in literature and art, and that he be acquainted with life and affairs, but the paramount qualification, after holiness of character, is that the minister should know his Bible. No accomplishments in Dogmatic Theology or Church History can ever compensate for ignorance of Holy Scripture. One might cheerfully sacrifice a multitude of dates, and a wealth of theories to make St. Luke's Gospel a part of his being; he has indeed done poorly for his people if he feeds them with the conclusions of Church Councils, instead of the abiding truths of St. John's Gospel. After all there is no theology so satisfying as Biblical, and the Acts of the Apostles are the seed-plot of all Church History. The most perfectly equipped pastor is he who knows the Bible from beginning to end in its by-paths as well as its main roads, in its underlying principles as well as its majestic sayings—who has its books arranged in their historical order and assigned

THE CONSTRUCTION OF THE BOOK 23

to their various provinces of life, who can distinguish between the temporary form which is secondary, and the Eternal Gospel which is the burden of its message, who can detect the correspondence between the word of the Lord in each period of Bible History and the environment of life, and can recognize a similar correspondence in our own day. He has fulfilled one of the chief conditions of successful preaching who can correlate a living book and a living age.

The Bible differs from every text-book of religion in that it is not a book, but a literature, and a preacher must understand its construction—not merely how many volumes there are in the canon, and such like external details, but how this long literature came into being, in short its organic growth. It is at this point that criticism renders its special service, and earns the just gratitude of the preacher. No one can estimate too highly for practical purposes the work of those patient and reverent scholars, who take up this apparently heterogeneous and confused material and set it in order of time, who assign it to the most likely authors, and connect it with the most congenial periods, who catch at each variation the governing note, and at each change focus the vision. An American scholar has said that "the price which the world has to pay for a great book is the labour of understanding it," and the contribution of criticism to the pulpit is to edit the book for practical use. The relation of the critic and the minister is very much that of the physiologist and the physician, and they ought to be on good terms. If there has been any misunderstanding it should be cleared up without delay, and this is not a hopeless task. The suspicion which fell on criticism, and still shadows it in the minds of pious people, is due, partly to the change it works in preconceived ideas of the form of the Bible, and partly to the standpoint of certain critics. The first ground is surely unreasonable, because so far as criticism convinces the readers of the Bible that its substance passed through the minds of living men and had a real meaning for its own generation, the Book gains enormously, both in lucidity and authority. But the other ground cannot be so lightly dismissed, for the standpoint of the critic is a most serious question. If he approaches the study of Holy Scripture with this principle either distinctly laid down, or working from the background of his mind, that it does not and cannot differ in any way from other literature —that the books of Moses and of Herodotus, that Plato and Isaiah, that Marcus Aurelius and St. Paul, are to be explained in exactly the same way; in short that the Bible as a matter of course has come into existence on ordinary conditions, and that no extraordinary influence may be admitted, then the critic will labour under a blinding and fettering disability. His eyes will be holden as he goes along the way by which God has travelled down the ages, so that he shall not be able to realize His presence. The signs of the divine he will deny by referring them to some lower cause; the impressions of the divine he will resist, and call them delusions because he starts with the dogma, that the book, wherever it came from, cannot have come from God. And there is no dogmatist so stiff and arrogant as an unbelieving critic. He is enslaved by his principle of agnosticism, and will apply it remorselessly to the interpretation of the Bible. Any unique event will be incredible, any unparalleled personage will be unhistorical; the visions will be translated into prose, and the magnificence of the book reduced to commonplace, till the prophets become unknown Jews with a genius for religious writing, and Jesus a gifted but self-deluded peasant of Galilee. There is a Spanish proverb: "If you desire to find gold in the Indies, you must bring it with you." If one comes to this book certain that he will find no God, none will reveal Himself; if he lay it down that this book is only one among many books created by the religious instinct, that and nothing more will it be to him. The influence of this school upon the preacher is deadly; it will penetrate his soul like an atmosphere, it will paralyze his energy like a subtle poison in his veins. For him the Bible will now have no lift; it will open up no long distances. He will be daily hampered in the free use of the most glorious promises, because he has learned to believe that they are only of men and have not come from God, and he will be perpetually explaining away the spiritual meaning of Bible facts, in order to bring them into line with uninspired history. In this low temperature the preacher will sink into a student of Jewish annals, and a lecturer on comparative religion. When the unbelieving critic captures the pulpit he devastates the pew; the imagination of the people will die under this arid influence, and their faith be filched away. The Eternal Hope itself will wither in their hearts, and the Bible which once was the garment of the risen Lord, from whose very hem virtue went out, will be only the grave clothes of a dead Christ.

Just because one has a profound sense of the service which criticism has rendered to truth, he has the less hesitation in protesting against its tyranny and its abuse. If the Church should not be afraid to use the critic as a servant, neither should the Church allow herself to be browbeaten by him as a master.

28 THE CONSTRUCTION OF THE BOOK

The Church is a guardian of the Bible, the critic is only its editor; his province is the letter, he may not meddle with the spirit of the book. There is a danger that a swollen and omniscient criticism should break bounds, and become the dictator to faith. The temptation of all specialism is insubordination to knowledge as a whole; the weakness of all specialism is complacent ignorance of other departments. When one critic of our day reduces the teaching of Jesus to a few sayings, and another, full of new wine, denies any Epistles to St. Paul, one learns the limits of specialized scholarship, and the folly of giving a blank check to critics of irresponsible judgment. One waits for the critic who shall boldly say, as some have been hinting, that Jesus is only a lay figure on which a beautiful tradition has been draped, and that He never lived any more than He rose from the dead. We shall then have the supreme irony of a scholar sitting within his study, and proving to his own satisfaction from a microscopic examination of manuscripts that there never has been any Christ, while outside his airless study, if he had only ears to hear the tramp of innumerable feet, he would know that the risen and triumphant Christ had for twenty centuries been marching along the high road of history in the living Church which is His Body and His instrument, His evidence and His manifestation.

Criticism is not, however, monopolized by the school of unbelief. Over against Kuenen stands Robertson Smith, one of the great scholars and true believers of modern times, and believing criticism approaches the book with another and more scientific mind. It recognizes at the outset that this book, upon the face of it, by virtue of the place it has held in the judgment of religious people and the work it has wrought in the world, will likely move on another plane and present features of a different kind from other books of religion. This criticism, while applying as rigidly the processes of scholarship to the study of the book, and opening its windows still more unreservedly to the light of history, holds itself open to recognize and welcome the hand of God behind events, and to catch

His voice through the words of human speech. If this criticism assumes God, it is a reasonable assumption, and then its office is to show how God has spoken, not by unravelling the mystery of inspiration, but by setting in order the circumstances of the message. As God has spoken in many portions and in divers manners, and since a better understanding of the form will help us to a fuller acceptance of the spirit, it is the function of the critic to write an introduction to the books of Scripture. From him we learn by whom they came—the authors of the book, when they were written—the environment of the book, their special burden—the gospel of the book, their place in the order of revelation—their relation to Scripture history as a whole, and also their prophecy—the anticipation of Christ. Each book is orientated by the critic: like a stone it is set in its place in the arch, of which it forms a part, and of which the key-stone is Christ. When the critic has done his work with the resources of his knowledge and under the guidance of faith, he restores the book to the preacher with the spirit untouched, but with the letter illuminated, so that every portion of ancient Scripture yields for the pulpit more vivid illustrations, more accurate parallels, more telling lessons, more timely appeals. Will any one deny that when Prof. George Adam Smith has finished with the prophets, they are ten times more serviceable for the pulpit, or when Professor Ramsay has done his unique service for the Acts of the Apostles, the preacher approaches the beginning of church history, with a more understanding mind, and a more confident faith?

While criticism has a duty to all literature, it renders a special service to Holy Scripture, because this book stands by itself not merely in its inspiration, but also in its construction. It comes upon one as a surprise, because it is not what we would have expected if we were to judge it by comparison with other manuals of religion. Were one of us coming to the Bible for the first time—and there are moments when one desires this sensation, he would expect to find it a glorified hand-book of theology, with a chapter on the being of

God, another on the person of Jesus Christ, a third on the nature of man, and a fourth on the scheme of salvation, with other chapters on judgment and the future life, and such like subjects. The reader would be able to turn to a certain page and find in a succinct proposition the particular truth he was seeking and which he must believe. The book from the first word to the last would be of the same date in the same style, upon the same level of revelation and everywhere charged with the same authority. It would be in all its parts of equal value, and absolute perfection; it would be removed everywhere from the influence of human feeling and human frailty. This is the ideal of our books of authoritative religion, whether the thirty-nine articles of the Anglican Church or the confession of faith adopted by the Scots Kirk. This is the principle of the Koran and the sacred book of the Mormons. And although the Bible has been for long centuries in the hands of Christian folk, yet the idea still lurks in their mind, that if you look closely enough into the book, and somehow or other get rid of certain miscellaneous material, this is its plan and intention.

The fact that the Bible is not a divine catechism may suggest to the minds of religious preachers that they should not place such implicit confidence in teaching religion by propositions. There is a place for ordered and digested knowledge in religion as in science, and one pays a willing tribute to the ability, both spiritual and theological, with which the text-books of Christianity have been compended, but it should not be forgotten that the Bible which remains the first and last book of our religion, proceeds upon a different method. The Bible one sees in an instant, is historical not theological; it proceeds on the lines of action, not speculation; it teaches by illustration, not by propositions. It is a book of life, laying its scene in the market-place, not in the study, and affects the soul, not by the presentation of abstract doctrine, but by encompassing it with an atmosphere of grace. Ought not this method of instruction, so interesting, and winsome, so human and reasonable, to be the ideal of the pulpit, and is it impossible to make it the model of our Christian text-books, in Sunday-schools, and Bible classes, while reserving the study of theology for colleges, and other places of sacred learning?

One's next thought on this general survey of the Bible, is, that if the Bible had been given us, as people seem to imagine, from heaven, like the stone tables handed to Moses—an immediate, complete and final revelation of everything we need to know about God and man—it would have been a wonderful, but futile Book; something to be kept and worshipped as an idol, but which could never have been a light or a power in human life. It would have been as useless as if it had been written in a new language used in heaven, but unknown on earth. It would have been foreign to the human mind, and remained an exotic in human life; it would not have belonged to us, and could never have become a part of us; it would have had as much affinity to us as to the Martians or any other race of conscious beings. If our sacred Book was to possess the soul and guide the feet of man, it must be grown from heavenly seed in human soil, and come to the full corn under the showers and sunshine of human life. Revelation must not be sudden, but gradual, not foreign, but native; its principle must not be creation, but evolution; it must be not a theurgy, but an education; and it must culminate, not in a visitation of God but in an incarnation.

When it is suggested that the method of revelation is based on the principle of evolution, it is necessary at once to distinguish between two ideas of evolution. There is that idea, which supposes that man is the last result of a long process, rising step by step from the lowest form of life to his present nature, and that this process has been carried on by some inherent, but blind energy, and that his spiritual nature is a product of the same process. This is an unbelieving and unreasonable theory of evolution. There is another idea which accepts the process, but affirms a mind guiding and controlling it, and also insists that while a man's body may have been developed from the lower animals, his spiritual faculties have come from another world This latter conception is reasonable and spiritual, carrying with it the belief in God, who uses the principle of evolution, as He may use any other for His high ends and also the immortality of the soul, which has not sprung from the animals but has come from God. In the same way if we hold, as the facts seem to compel us, that revelation has been an evolution, we must distinguish between two readings of the word, one of faith, and one of unbelief. The critics of unbelief hold that there has been a gradual development of religious truth, rising from the primary, and rude ideas of the Hebrews to the teaching of Jesus, but they do not admit either the action of the divine Spirit, or a guiding purpose of God. The growth has been all natural in the sense that it has not been divine. But, when writers of this school try to discover the source of Bible literature, and especially the origin of the idea of God, they are at a loss and contra-

THE CONSTRUCTION OF THE BOOK

dict one another—Rénan, for example, insists on the monotheism of a Semitic people, while Kuenen rather lays stress on "Israel's peculiar fortunes." If the Bible be a natural evolution, then its spiritual energy and its spiritual goal are both inexplicable. The Book would then have no indwelling of God and no unity. But it does present an ever more convincing presence of the divine, and it moves steadily to the union of man and God in the Incarnation.

Revelation then is to be considered a spiritual evolution, by which the human soul is educated by God through the experience of God in life, till it rises to union with Him in Christ, when as it were the soul comes to the body of humanity. As we carry the whole past history of our physical self in our body, and science can trace in fleshy tablets the stages of our development, so the history of our spiritual self is written in the Bible, and can be followed from barbarism to sainthood; as the race ascends from the sheiks of the desert to the saints before the throne. Any one can see who reads his Bible with ordinary intelligence, that there has been a continual advance both in knowledge, and in conduct, from the patriarchs to the prophets, and from the prophets to the apostles, with many stages between. Take for instance the growth in the idea of God. There was first of all the original conception of the Eternal, as the "Lord"; this changes in the days of the patriarchs into the "Almighty," which marks an advance from the vague belief in a deity to the conception of a deity controlling nature. When Israel is delivered from Egypt, God receives a new name, "Jehovah," and people now think of God as coming forth and declaring Himself. By and by as the moral sense of the nation is developed, alike by the mercies and by the judgments of God, they learn to call Him, the "Holy One of Israel." The Deity is now invested with a spiritual character, and as time goes on, as prophet after prophet realizes God, and makes known his vision, this character is charged like a golden vessel, with righteousness, faithfulness, loving kindness and tender mercy. The later prophets are accustomed to refer to God under the majestic title of "Jehovah of Hosts," a name associated with the rise of the monarchy, and which the prophets used to assert their faith in the holiness and sovereignty, in the overwhelming glory, and victorious might of God. Another instance of growth can be found in the idea of sacrifice. Abraham, anxious to show his devotion to God and to give of his best, intends to offer his only son, according to the fashion of the day, and learns that while his devotion was acceptable, his action would be a crime. Instead of human sacrifice, beasts now become the symbol of penitence and consecration, and with the smoke of many sacrifices the prayers of men go up to God. Then the prophets begin to denounce sacrifice with scornful words, making the Eternal say, "To what purpose is the multitude of your sacrifices unto Me, saith the Lord; I am full of the burnt offerings of rams and the fat of fed beasts, and I delight not in the blood of bullocks or of lambs or of he goats." Those offerings were formal and elementary, they were not worthy of God to whom they were offered, or of man who offered them. There was a better gift to be laid upon the altar and a more spiritual consecration to be accomplished, and the voice of an anonymous writer is heard, "Sacrifice and offering Thou did'st not desire, my ears hast Thou opened; burnt offering and sin offering hast Thou not required. Then said I, lo I come, in the volume of the book it is written of me, I delight to do Thy will, O God, yea Thy law is within my heart." When the second Isaiah wrote, there had arisen before the imagination of prophecy, a holy and meek Victim, who is the Servant of the Lord, and by His sufferings makes atonement for the nation. And the idea of sacrifice reaches its lonely and radiant height, when in the great tragedy of history, Jesus offers Himself a sacrifice of obedience to the divine will, upon the cross of Calvary, and opens up the new way unto God the Father. "One other instance of progress from the lower to the higher idea may be found"—I am now quoting from Illingworth's admirable

Bampton Lectures, " Personality, Human and Divine "—" in the process by which man has come to recognize what we call his personality, all that is potentially or actually contained within himself—in a word what it means to be a man." When Jephthah devotes his daughter to death or to the celibate religious life, according as you interpret the passage, or parents offer their own children with hideous cruelty unto Moloch; when whole families or whole tribes are punished together for the ill-doing of one, it is plain that the individual was at the disposal of his family or merged in his nation. The individual has no rights and no separate existence. He has hardly the right to say I; he can hardly be said to have a separate existence in those early days. The prophets themselves dealt with Israel as a whole and called the nation the servant of the Lord; they make little of individuality and hardly address themselves to the individual. It was Christ who found the individual, because He revealed the true and divine conception of personality. In Christ men realized themselves, in Christ they understood themselves, in Christ they became strong and free. And so the Christian Apostle writes, " I live, yet not I, but Christ liveth in me."

While revelation is steadily advancing, and the idea of God, of religion, of man, is growing deeper and clearer, the progress is towards a fixed goal. From the beginning one can see with the complete Bible in his hands, that the book is moving towards Christ, as the physical evolution has risen to man. While the Fathers of the Church were certainly too fond of allegorizing, and one's reason does not welcome the doctrine of the Holy Trinity in any casual combination of three persons in Bible history, and while many pious Divines of last century were too fond of spiritualizing the incidents of Bible history, yet it is true that, as from the furthest confine of the Roman Empire there ran a road to Rome, so from the end of Holy Scripture there is a way to Christ. The two Testaments correspond, and the New Testament is the climax and the key of the Old. The types of the early dispensation which are not to be despised by the preacher (and on which the best book still remains that of Principal Fairbairn), all shadow Christ. The promises of divine mercy and help, which illuminate the toilsome and tragic road of revelation, all travel towards Christ. The great heroes of Hebrew history become transfigured, and raised to heroic size, like shapes in a luminous mist, and are associated with the coming Messiah; the spiritual imagination of saints, praying for the golden age and longing for a perfect humanity, reach forward to Christ, whom not having seen they love. Throughout the Old Testament there is what may be called an instinct of Christ, as when the sea bird makes for the ocean. There is an unconscious demand for Him, there is a growing expectation of Him at last, there is an eager waiting till He come. Without Christ the Bible had been a dark riddle, and the education of the race had missed its crown; with Christ the Bible is an open secret, and a long purpose of grace has been fulfilled. Christ is the culmination of the spiritual evolution.

There have been certain high water marks

in the history of man, where a tidal wave has left its visible traces upon the sands of time. Possibly the human intellect has never risen so high, or achieved such works, as in the fifth century before Christ in Greece. No dramatist has surpassed Sophocles, no philosopher can be compared with Socrates, no statesman has arisen more brilliant than Pericles, no artists are to be compared with the men who adorned the Acropolis. Like solitary Alps those names, with others of the same period, stand unapproachable. That golden age of letters and of art shows the possibility of humanity, to it the race is slowly and painfully rising, by it the mind of man is to be estimated and judged. After the same fashion the high water mark of spiritual life was reached by Christ and the writers of the New Testament Scriptures, who were especially filled with His Spirit and afford the most unshadowed reflection of His character. In His life and work, and most of all in Himself, His beautiful and perfect personality, have been fulfilled all the anticipations of saints and prophets, exceeding abundantly

THE CONSTRUCTION OF THE BOOK 45

above all that they asked or thought; in Him are realized all the hopes and imaginations, the desires and ambitions of the human soul when it stands upon its highest places, and holds its most intimate communion with God. Short of Him revelation could not stop, beyond Him revelation cannot go. There is nothing to be conceived and nothing to be craved in the province of the soul above Christ. As there is in the recesses of the human mind an ideal of perfect physical beauty, which one could not describe, but which is satisfied when one looks upon the Apollo Belvedere or the Hermes which was found not long ago in Greece, so in the recesses of the human soul there is an idea of spiritual beauty, which the writers of the Old Testament struggled to portray, but which is realized with exceeding glory in Jesus Christ. The presentation of Christ is both the glorification and the vindication of the Bible. When we look upon the picture of that bright excellency, we forget the fashion of the frame, and do not ask the name of the painter; the living Christ as He stands out in relief from the gospel records is independent of criticism. Were the Bible to be destroyed as a unique picture might be burned in some catastrophe, that face would remain engraven upon the heart of every one who had seen it, and be transmitted unto those who came after. No prophet and no poet could have created Christ; He is the anointed of God, whom the ages had seen afar off, and stretched out their hands to embrace. He is the visible shape of God, and it is not, in the last issue, the Bible which proves Christ, but Christ who proves the Bible.

This conception of the method of revelation—as a gradual and orderly evolution of truth, under the guidance of the divine Spirit, till it culminates in Christ—can be used by the preacher for two practical ends. And the first is the defense of Bible ethics. Every minister, in what I may call large practice, receives a certain number of letters a year, from persons who cannot accept the Bible as a revelation of God or a guide of conduct, for some such reasons as the following: that Jacob cheated Esau out of his birthright; that many of the inhabitants of Canaan were put to the sword; that David was the chosen of the Lord, and lived licentiously; that Samuel hewed Agag to pieces to win the approval of God. Popular writers of the unbelieving school enlarge with indignant eloquence and a strong appeal to the moral sense, upon the low standard of morals in the Old Testament, and upon the glaring crimes committed by religious men. It is unjust to say that those critics are captious and prejudiced; we are bound to believe that they are seeking for the light, and that they have found certain incidents in Old Testament history a grave offense to their consciences. What then is the advocate of faith to say, and how is he not merely to meet objections by plausible answers, but, which is far better, to remove stumbling-blocks from his brother's path? With all respect for the teachers of the past, it may be admitted that they did not always take the most convincing or the most ingenuous line of argument. They were apt to excuse the conduct of good men and to cover up their faults; they deeply resented any reflection on the lives of the patriarchs, or any criticism of what seemed to be done by the command of God. They held as it were a brief for Jacob and his kind and defended him like a low class criminal barrister in a police court. They were also inclined to take high and dangerous ground about the rights of God, asserting that He could do as He pleased with His creatures, and that if He ordered any one to be put to death, this execution was justified by the fact that His life was at God's disposal. They had the courage indeed to credit the Eternal with deeds which in justice they would have been ashamed to commit themselves, and for which they would have been brought before the nearest magistrate. This line of apologetics was thoroughly bad, because it perverted the reason and debauched the conscience, and it was only adopted because our predecessors held the theory that the Bible was on the same plane of revelation from beginning to end; that what was done in Genesis was as absolutely right as what was done in the Gospels, and that a text from Genesis was as valuable for building doctrine as a saying of Jesus. With our principle of evolution we are able to take up stronger ground, and to repel attacks upon the Bible morality with confidence, and to remove objections from the minds of honest men. The Bible contains the history of morality, as it rose from level to level, for it has been as much a growth as the knowledge of God. Indeed the revelation of truth and the revelation of conduct have kept step; just as the idea of God was imperfect, so was the standard of character; when the idea of God came to its height, the perfection of character was revealed. Morality, crystallized in the Ten Commandments, is spiritualized in the Sermon on the Mount. When any one therefore denounces the ethics of the Bible, let us ask the date of the incident. Upon the date rests the defense. So many centuries before Christ? That gives a new complexion and demands a different judgment. What one asks now is not whether this thing would be done by Christian men, but only whether it was appreciably more moral than the average morality of the day. A Christian government would not put a nation to the sword as the Hebrews put the Canaanites, but other nations around in that day were doing the same thing, with this difference, that while they did it through sheer brutality, the Hebrews did it in the interest of morality; because the vices of Canaan were so beastly they cleansed the land by blood. From our standpoint it was an atrocity, from their standpoint it was an act of justice. The Hebrews of that time had developed a conscience which hated impurity even unto death, and therefore revelation at that date was vindicated. One must also ask the censor of the Bible whether it is fair to judge any process before it is complete. When the picture has received its last touch, and the book has passed finally from the printer's hands, and the building has been roofed in, and the cloth is ready for the market, you are entitled to approve or condemn. It is foolish and it is not fair to descend upon the work in the course of making, for the very faults you condemn may disappear before its completion. What can any one say

THE CONSTRUCTION OF THE BOOK 51

against the ethic of the Bible when it has come to its full height, and that is not in the book of Judges but in the four Gospels? Has any one the heart, and has any one the courage to complain of the ideal laid down by Christ, and exemplified in His life? It is not by Jacob but by St. Paul, not by Jael but by the Madonna, it is not by the rude soldiers of early days, but by Jesus of Nazareth that the Bible stands or falls. The Bible comes to its flower in the Sermon on the Mount.

Our age is inclined to offer another and subtler objection to the ethic of the Bible, and that is not that it is too low, but that it is too high. The stress is laid now, not on the conduct of people centuries before Christ—talk which may be treated charitably and which indeed is not much worse than can be expected of the average man to-day—but upon the model set up by Jesus in His teaching, and illustrated in His own life. The Christian life, say those apostles of the commonplace and eulogists of pedestrian morality, is in the clouds and not upon the earth, a life unpractical, impossible, futile, although most beautiful. They kneel to Christ in order to renounce allegiance; they applaud Christ in order to remove Him from practical politics; they bow to Him as they show Him to the door. If you press them for reasons, they give the example of His poverty, His demands for service, the spirituality of His commandments, and the meekness of temper which He makes a characteristic of His kingdom. If any one, they say, were to act as Christ directs, he would have to go out of this world, and become a monk, and the law of Christ could hardly be kept even then; for the man who has to toil and spin to get daily bread for himself and for other people, to manage his affairs and also the affairs of a nation, the ideals of Christ are not only vain but destructive. It may be suggested in passing that this objector had not distinguished between the call which Christ gave to His apostles, and which He gives to certain in every age, to leave all because they are called to special service, and the call which comes to ordinary folk who serve their Lord within their homes, and within the province of daily duty. Perhaps Catholic theology has been wiser than Protestant and more in touch with facts, in allowing two orders of service and two degrees of sainthood. When the young ruler declined the call of Christ, he did not refuse to be a Christian, or else no man can be a Christian unless he deprives himself of property and enters on the life of poverty; he refused to join the little band of men who had broken every worldly tie in order to found the kingdom of God.

Without, however, pressing that point, the preacher can find two answers to this objection of hopeless perfection. Surely for one thing it is a tribute to the splendour of the Bible ethics and the lonely supremacy of Christ. Is it not an honour to Christianity that it has set so lofty a standard and made so exacting a demand? If Christianity should fail, because it has dared so much, it will be high failure; if Christianity should succeed, because it asked little, it would be poor success. Suppose Christ made a primrose path for our tender feet, instead of the hard way of the cross; suppose He brought His religion nearly down to the level of a decent life, and made no difference between being a Christian and living the worldly life; suppose He coaxed and compromised and levelled down, and yielded, would He have commanded our honour, and would He have obtained our loyalty? One may refuse to pay a high price for a picture because he cannot afford it; he may also refuse to pay a low price, because the picture is not worth anything. One would not care to join even a club which received every applicant, and where your companions would be disreputable people, or an insurance company which had a large body of policy holders, because it took every worthless life. We are not really heartened when the ideal set before us is paltry; we do our best when the ideal is the most sublime. It were better to die trying to be a Christian, than to live having succeeded in being a Pharisee. Christianity is a splendid endeavour, even though it may sometimes be a hopeless despair; in its very difficulty and elevation lie its greatness and its success.

THE CONSTRUCTION OF THE BOOK 55

> "That low man seeks a little thing to do,
>   Sees it and does it;
> This high man, with a great thing to pursue,
>   Dies e'er he knows it.
> That low man goes on adding one to one,
>   His hundreds soon hit;
> This high man, aiming at a million,
>   Misses a unit."

But there is another answer to this charge of disheartening perfection, and it is full of hope. We must take Christ's teaching as a whole, and we must take Christ as He is. It is a mistake to pick and choose among His words, or to divide up His character. If He gave stringent commandments, He accompanied them by most gracious promises, and if He presented Himself as a model, He also offered Himself as a Saviour. The ideal which he held out to His disciple in His life, He died in order to make real. He is not, according to the Bible idea, an unapproachable and unique figure, but the type of humanity; not a height which can never be climbed by any other feet, but the true stature of Christianity. No doubt He is raised high above His most spiritual and heavenly disciples, but after Him they strive and pant and Him they also suggest, and illustrate. This great thing cannot be done in a day. It was a long time before Christ came, and a very arduous progress; it may be a long time before humanity is like Christ, and a severe discipline; but the Bible is not a flat surface, it has a large atmosphere and a far perspective; it is not confined to time, it moves in the region of eternity. St. Paul was not a fool when he described even Corinthian Christians as saints; he imagined what they were going to be; he was not raving when he wrote about all spiritual blessings in heavenly places, he was prophesying. Christ is not the condemnation but the salvation of humanity.

We ought also to apply this principle of the evolution of revelation to the development of truth. As Christ showed us in His life what we ought to be, He taught us in His words what we need to know; but just as it may be long before we have attained to the character of Christ, it may be as long before we have assimilated the knowledge of Christ.

During His earthly ministry He gave the substance of truth, but only in the sense in which the acorn includes the oak. Since that day the truth has been growing in the consciousness of His disciples, and under the teaching of His spirit. In one sense the Bible is complete, and no book can be added, because no one can pass Christ. In another sense the Bible is still being written and many books being added, because the teaching of Christ is bearing new harvests every age. The Acts of the Apostles break off abruptly, but they have not been concluded. They are indeed the fifth Gospel, the Gospel of the Holy Ghost, and it is still being written. It will not be complete till the end of the age and the coming of the Lord, when His work has been completed and a perfect humanity presented to the Father. There is a correspondence between the teaching of Jesus and the circumstances of periods, and the Spirit of Christ leads His disciples into truth in a progressive and orderly fashion. For it does not follow that because Christ gave many truths they can all be developed contemporaneously. They are together in the gospels, but they will flower one after the other, according to their proper season in human history. When you arrange your window box at the beginning of winter, you place in the hospitable soil snowdrops, crocuses, tulips, and hyacinths. They lie together in the kindly earth, receiving the same showers and the same sunshine; then appear first the snowdrops, harbingers of spring, followed by the richness of the crocuses; after them come the tulip, and last of all the fragrant and graceful hyacinths. Their planting was contemporaneous, their flowering was progressive. One recognizes that while Christ told His diciples all things, the Spirit brings them after a wise order to the disciples' remembrance. There is no doubt that Christ laid down the principle of human brotherhood, but if the Apostles had gone up and down the world preaching the emancipation of the slaves, society would have been shaken to its foundations, and government would have sunk into anarchy. It was in a later day that this application of the principle could be safely made, and it can never be applied rashly. Jesus taught the Fatherhood of God, but when in the first centuries of the Christian era, civilization was falling to pieces under the corruption of vice, and the decay of reverence, men needed to learn the sovereignty and the righteousness of God. Within our own memory we have seen the sterner conception of the Almighty as a judge, yield to the more beautiful idea of Him as a Father, and have recognized that the spirit of Jesus has been guiding the Church. Christian men of last century had a very imperfect sense of the responsibility of wealth, and their duty as stewards of the gift of God. To-day, the words of Jesus are coming out before men's eyes, like secret writing brought beneath the heat of the sun, and society is already studying with friendly interest and unfeigned admiration, the most altruistic sayings of Jesus. What a hundred years ago would have been judged hopelessly ideal in His teaching, is now becoming real. Millionaires write upon the gospel of wealth and give earnest thought how they can denude themselves of their possessions, in order to help their fellow men. With every century some truth which Christ taught shall come into season, and bear its fruit, and therefore while other literatures lose their hold and perish, while systems of theology and philosophy rise and fall, the Bible remains through all the generations and all the changes. This Book has once been written, but is ever being fulfilled; it is contemporaneous with all the centuries, and in touch at every point with human life, because it is the revelation of the living God. Because God lives, the Bible lives; because God works, the Bible works. There is in it the breath of God: "The grass withereth, the flower fadeth, but the word of our God shall stand forever."

LECTURE II
THE STANDPOINT OF THE BOOK

LECTURE II

THE STANDPOINT OF THE BOOK

IF one would catch the likeness in a portrait, he must stand at the proper angle of light; if one would gather the secret treasure of a book, he must enter into its intention. Every department of thought has its own province, and every book has its own motive. With science it is the study of the facts of nature; with literature it is the criticism of life; with philosophy it is the principle of things; with art it is the appreciation of beauty. One book may no doubt travel in various spheres—Huxley, who had a profound respect for the Bible, expounded science in the most lucid English, and Ruskin, who was richly fed upon the Bible, was as much distinguished by his brilliant style, as by his artistic insight. There have been authors who seem to embrace the universe of knowledge, and to be cosmopolitan in their writing, but it remains that every book has its inherent bias, and its visible direction. It is fair that a book be judged by its execution; it is imperative that it be judged by its intention. If one knows not for what end the book was conceived and created, then he will be as a stranger, wandering round some ancient cathedral, and guessing at the scenes upon the painted glass. If one has the key then he enters in at the door, and possesses the interior at his pleasure, while the light streams in upon him through the rich and mellow glory of the ancient glass.

Beyond all books, the Bible is an engaging but hopeless mystery to the outsider, while it yields its secret to the man who is within. Because people have not always tried to find the standpoint of the Bible, but have been content with confused notions about it, they have not been able to use it with confidence, but have fumbled over its meaning. No book has been so unjustly attacked, no book has been so foolishly defended, and for this the blame must be divided between its foes and its friends, neither of whom have in many cases taken the trouble to search out and firmly grasp its controlling purpose.

It may be urged in the excuse of both that on the surface the Bible does not seem to be a unity, in the same sense as a catechism is, or a drama. What one looks out upon is not a study of any side of humanity, but humanity in its vastness; not the survey of a province of life, but life in its variety; not botanical specimens, dried and pressed, presented in the cases of a museum, but the hillside in summer time, where the flowers are growing in reckless profusion and every contrast of colour. The reader is plunged into an ocean of human details. The love affairs of a man and a maid and contracts of marriage; the quarrels between brothers with their treachery and their revenge; the bargains in business, wherein land is bought and sold, and covenants are made with witnesses; the feuds between rival tribes, enlivened by raids and captures; the choice of kings and their anointing amid the rejoicing of the people; the evil doing of kings and their assassination amid a people's hatred; the orations of statesmen as they warn their nation against offending God, or comfort them in days of tribulation; adroit arrangements of ecclesiastics, and the inner history of church councils; the collision of parties in the Christian Church, and the bitter rivalries which distract congregations; the radiant record of deeds of chivalry, and the black story of acts of treachery—the romance of unselfish friendship, and the blind enmity of religious bigotry; the career of a successful man, and the unmerited suffering of a martyr; the devotion of a mother to her child, and the jealousy of women fighting for the same man's love; the idyll of childhood; the strength of young manhood, the mellow wisdom of old age—nomads of the desert, dwellers in the city; prophets and sages, ploughmen and vine-dressers, soldiers and traders, rich men and beggars, holy matrons and women who are sinners; patriarchs driving huge herds before them, and apostles going forth with nothing in their hands; priests offering sacrifice in the holy place,

THE STANDPOINT OF THE BOOK 67

and publicans collecting their gains in the receipt of custom; scholars busy in their studies, and carpenters toiling in their shop— all pass across this stage in unarranged and natural procession. Nothing could be more artless, nothing more fascinating. This is a larger and more vivid Shakespeare; but wherefore? Is there any more connection between all the volumes that make this literature than between thirty novels selected from different periods and nations? It is a gorgeous kaleidoscope, but does it leave one definite impression?

Upon a second and more careful reading of the literature one is conscious of a certain spirit which is informing and harmonizing every part, like a system of nerves, and making all the members of the body one. The story of the patriarchs is not recorded in Genesis because they were successful stock farmers, but because they were the pioneers in the quest of the soul for God. There is this difference between the life of Joseph, who rose from being a slave to be prime minister, and the triumphant biography of self-made men, with which material ambition is somewhat coarsely fed, that the crisis in Joseph's life was his victory over temptation, and the glory of his life was not his success, but his character. From first to last the career of Moses was a romance, but his sterling point is his preference of the unseen above the seen, and his identification with the suffering people of God, whereby, according to a felicitous stroke of Bible genius, he esteemed "the reproach of Christ greater riches than the treasures of Egypt." Joshua was a resolute soldier, but the victory which crowned his arms was due to his unshaken and single-hearted faith in God. The prophets were in many cases able statesmen, and they were always forceful writers, but they have owed their immortality to their spiritual vision and their fellowship with the Eternal. The psalmists were poets of the grand order, but they seized the heart of humanity because they have sung the epic of the soul. The line of David is continued because he feared God, but the line of Jeroboam, the son of Nebat, came to an end because he made

Israel to sin. As you travel down Old Testament history you may find yourself in strange byways, but sooner or later you are brought face to face with God. The writers are intent upon one thing, and that is righteousness; they are ever seeking for one person, and that is God. There is not only a progress, but it is a progress upwards; from the valley the path climbs the hillside, till it reaches the finer and rarer air of the gospels, where we are living in the outer court of eternity, and at the gate of heaven. The innumerable details of the Book are only its body; the living soul of the Book is religion, the fellowship of man with God. We lay aside the history which is but the stalk and the leaf of the plant; we garner the grain, which is the revelation of God. One purpose governs and illuminates, invigorates and glorifies the Bible, and that is spiritual. It is the supreme Book of religion.

The religious spirit of the Book is proved by the way in which the historical incidents have lent themselves to spiritual experience so that through the screen of ordinary life the eternal light has been shining. The journey of the children of Israel from Egypt to Canaan has been the ever fresh and unfailing illustration of the chief pilgrimage of man, when he escapes from the bondage of sin and the tyranny of his senses, and takes his toilsome way through the heat and weariness of the desert, fed by the bread which came down from heaven, and the water that has flowed from a stricken Christ till he passes through the dark waters of death and enters into his land of promise. The kingdom of Israel, with its anointed king, and its chosen capitol of Jerusalem, with its tragic sufferings and exile, with its amazing deliverances and triumphs, is the figure of the Church of God, with her head at the right hand of the Father, and her home in the heavenly city, the New Jerusalem, as she sins and suffers, believes and attains through the checkered annals of the centuries. It is a true and profound instinct which finds in the Seventy-second Psalm, whoever wrote it and to whomsoever it first referred, the prophecy of the Prince whose kingdom would be righteousness, peace, and joy, in whom the victims of life would find their deliverer, and the needy their helper, which identifies in the sufferings of exiled Israel the servant of the Lord, the forerunner of Him who was "despised and rejected of men"; who was "wounded for our transgressions, bruised for our iniquities." St. Paul also has in the judgment of all men, pierced to the heart of things when he lifts the life and death of Christ from the level of simple martyrdom, and the common circumstances of Nazareth and Calvary, to the height of a spiritual drama, wherein His disciples after a mystical fashion suffer and die with Him, rise and are glorified with Him.

This august Book is forever before the minds of men—it is as inevitable as Christ; it is ever being judged by men, it is as arresting as Christ. For indeed it is the Christ within the Book which is its soul, and the Christ presented in the Book who is judge. No minister of the word should complain because the Bible is ever in debate, for this only proves its vitality and its supremacy. If no book has ever been so loved, none has ever been more hated; if no book has ever been so valued, none has ever been so depreciated. It was in the beginning of its history that Lucian declared Christianity to be "the latest folly in the world's madhouse," and late in its history that Voltaire allowed himself to describe the Bible as "A tissue of fables fit only for cobblers and tailors." But the Bible has pursued its triumphant way and to-day is translated into more dialects, and read by more people than any other book. It deals generously both with its foes and with its friends. As the arch of triumph in Paris preserves the name of obscure villages because the French won victories there, so writers on whose volumes the dust is lying thick, have obtained a dubious immortality, because they attacked the Bible; and if any one theologian or preacher has grace enough to absorb its spirit, its life will pass into his words, and at the least its words will adorn his writings as with a thread of gold upon his hodden gray. This literature makes only one volume, but it beyond all other literatures

THE STANDPOINT OF THE BOOK

combined, of ancient and of modern times, has inspired poets, artists, scholars, patriots, besides creating the doctors and heralds of the gospel. It is an easy task therefore to defend the Bible, and to beat back every assault, but the highest line of apology is not its invincible position, or its magnificent circulation, not its graphic style, nor its overflowing humanity. The Bible must stand or fall as a book of religion. It is important to show that the Bible has illuminated men's minds, and made them lovers of knowledge, that it has strengthened men's hearts and given them a passion for freedom; that it has renewed their morals, and filled them with respect for righteousness; that it has touched their emotions, and set up an altar to pity in every place where it has come. But if with all this service, it has not revealed God, so that He may be known to men, and has not invested Him with grace, so that He may be loved; if it has not brought the soul by a new and living way into the Holy Place of the Eternal, then the Bible has failed of its chief end. But if this

Book has lifted the veil from the face of God so that men can call Him their friend, their strength, their portion, their Saviour, their Father, then the Bible has succeeded in its high mission. For the God which is in us is placed in communication with the God which is in the Book, and through the revelation contained in Holy Scripture, the soul has intimate commerce with its Maker.

"Speak to Him thou, for He hears, and spirit with spirit can meet;
Closer is He than breathing, and nearer than hands and feet."

Because it unveils God, and releases the soul, because through its ministry God and man are brought near; the Book is not only justified but glorified. "I have found in it," said a great thinker in the "Confessions of an Inquiring Spirit," "words for my inmost thoughts, songs for my joy, utterance for my hidden griefs, and pleadings for my shame and feebleness. In short whatsoever finds me, bears witness for itself that it has proceeded from the Holy Spirit."

THE STANDPOINT OF THE BOOK

The preacher therefore in his use of the Bible should disentangle its chief purpose which is that of grace, from other ends which it may more or less imperfectly serve. For instance it was never intended to be a handbook of history. With the exception of St. Luke, there is hardly any writer who understands historical technique, and there is hardly an attempt to present a consistent and orderly narrative from the days of the patriarchs to the coming of Christ. Different narratives of the same event are included without explanation or harmony. Various authors are allowed to describe periods or characters from different standpoints. There are traces of many documents and many minds, of conflicts between schools and interests.

No one should rest the authority of the Bible upon its dates, or upon its figures. He is not really dealing with a compact and correct little primer of ancient history, but with an independent and dramatic literature. Surely the day is past when devout people will treat the fall as a literal transaction, and base upon it, as Dutch theologians used to do, a vast and cumbrous system of Covenant theology with conditions and seals and whatnot, as in a document drawn up by an attorney. If ever there was a profound and searching, as well as beautiful and convincing spiritual poem, it is the story of the Garden of Eden. We know that the chapters of innocence, temptation, sin, and sorrow are true, because they happen in every one's life, as through selfwill we also lose our Eden and go out upon our wander-year. It is not with incredible history, but with spiritual experience, the Book opens. Why should the preacher therefore be troubled, if errors in arithmetic, or contradictions in accounts be discovered in the Bible, and brought as a charge against its reliability? The question is not its accuracy in statistics, but its reality in religion. Does it matter that the Garden of Eden cannot be identified by a traveller, if it can be found in a man's life? Why then should the preacher weary his people with maps of Jewish battle-fields, and catalogues of Jewish kings? Why should he

THE STANDPOINT OF THE BOOK 77

toil to the torture of his mind and the withering of his soul, trying to spiritualize geography and genealogy? Is it not a waste to spend so much time and trouble upon the chronicles and customs of the Jews, beyond what is necessary for the understanding of the prophetical writings, and the allusions of the New Testament? It does seem a futility that excellent men of old should have occupied years of preaching in explaining the minutiæ of Jewish sacrifices and that children's memories should have been laden with the names of the kings of Israel, when the gospels were an inexhaustible deep, and the romantic story of the Christian Church lay ready for the telling. It struck one that certain ministers seemed more at home in the book of Numbers than in the Sermon on the Mount, and had more interest in showing how the tabernacle was constructed than expounding the principles of the Kingdom of God. The spirit was smothered by the letter, and the ritual of the Jewish Temple which surely is only of very secondary importance incroached upon the teaching of Jesus, which ought to be the commanding theme of the Christian ministry. History is only the rough casket which conceals the jewel, only the temporary scaffolding within which the building is erected.

Ought not the preacher also to fix in the minds of his people that the Bible was never intended to be a book of science, and to save his people from those absurd panics about the conflict between science and faith, which have made the Church ridiculous. One does not know whether it is more absurd, for blundering apologists to twist the language of Holy Scripture so as to show that its references to nature are really in keeping with the last discoveries of science, and that in fact they have been a cryptogram, or to insist that science in the result of its investigations has contradicted the literal statements of Holy Scripture, and therefore has wantonly and blasphemously attacked the revelation of God. It is pitiable to remember the catalogue of conflicts wherein the Church has left her own ground and, invading a foreign province, has invariably been defeated and put to shame. When Copernicus made his great discovery that the earth went round the sun, and not the sun round the earth, the Church raged furiously, and scientists under threat of death had to deny the fact. But the solar system is indifferent to criticism and the earth went on her course in spite of the resolutions of theologians, and to-day the most timid Christian is not dismayed, when he reads in his Bible that the sun arose or set any more than he feels obliged to apologize when he uses the same popular language himself. The religious world was thrown into confusion last century by the celebrated "Vestiges of Creation" which was published anonymously, but is now understood to have been written by Robert Chambers, because "the action of general laws was traced throughout the universe as a system of growth and development, and it was argued that the various species of animals and plants had been produced in orderly succession from each other by the action of unknown laws of development aided by the action of external conditions." This was regarded as a direct assault upon the Mosaic account of the creation, and an insidious denial of the Creator. Hugh Miller, the geologist, came to the aid of the theologian, and it may be urged in excuse of the attitude taken up by the Church, that geologists, like Sir Charles Lyell, and naturalists like Professor Agassiz repudiated the conclusions of Mr. Chambers. It was not discreditable in that pre-Darwinian age that theologians should have refused to accept the new theory, since they were only keeping step with some of the most distinguished scientists; it was simply unfortunate that they rushed into the controversy with which they had nothing to do, and bound up the authority of revelation with a theory of the creation. Later in the same century Darwin brought out his "Origin of Species," and just as Newton by his demonstration of the law of gravitation laid a sure foundation for all future study of the starry heavens, so Darwin by his discovery of the law of natural selection established a firm foundation for all future study of nature.

THE STANDPOINT OF THE BOOK 81

As this discovery, however, replaced the idea of a special creation, and as Christian teachers had still fettered themselves to the position that Moses was an inspired writer of natural history, Darwin was denounced by the pulpit from the rising to the setting sun. Perhaps the height of foolishness was touched when at a meeting of the British Association, Bishop Wilberforce condemned Darwin, who could have taught that ambitious prelate a lesson in unworldliness, and Darwin's views which he did not understand, with "inimitable spirit, emptiness and unfairness." The Bishop who had provoked Huxley that day beyond endurance was soundly trounced by that uncompromising speaker, and one may safely say that no accredited and intelligent defender of the Bible would repeat the Bishop's mistake. We have come to understand that it is not for us to dictate to the Eternal, how He should have brought His world into being, whether by acts of separate creation or by a process of evolution, and that if we desire information upon His ways in nature, we must turn not to the pages of

Moses, but to the laboratories of the scientist. We have, it is to be hoped, thrown off that conception of the Old Testament, which is illustrated in the Jewish Kabbala, and which makes the Book an inspired encyclopedia wherein you can inquire on science, philosophy, and every department of human knowledge. May we also hope that we are escaping from the uncalled-for task of reconciling science and religion, which is very much the same as reconciling physiology and astronomy, and that in future the preacher of the gospel will confine himself to the concerns of the soul and leave the student of nature freedom in his own province. The evangelist and the scientist move along parallel lines, and neither has any right to deny the other. As knowledge grows the lines may approximate, and one day meet, as God and man have been united in the Incarnation, wherein a perfect soul from heaven and a perfect body from earth have formed the one Person of the Lord.

It may be useful for the preacher to guard himself against that interesting view of the

Bible, which regards it as simply a strenuous and beautiful literature. Certainly it is a literature and in our English translation has done more than any other book to sustain the standard of style, and to feed the springs of inspiration. But the good is often the enemy of the best, and just as the elements in the sacrament of Holy Communion have in the speculation of theology overshadowed the presence of the Lord, and just as the beauty of public worship in ancient buildings, and by elaborate ritual, have been apt to diminish its spirituality, so if the mind be too much occupied with the literary form of the Bible it may become less susceptible to its inward grace. It is of course absurd that young people should be trained in the classics of Greece and Rome, and not introduced to the magnificence of Holy Scripture, as a discipline of culture, and a standard of imagination. It would also correct some of the more pedantic vagaries of the Higher Criticism if the canons of literature were brought to bear upon their work, and they were induced to treat the book as a human document, and the good taste of religious people would be raised, and preaching as well as prayer would be delivered from many vulgarities and stupidities if the minds of ministers were saturated with the literary spirit of the Bible, and their speech was based upon its grand style. More attention should be given to the literary study of the Bible, and I will take this opportunity of recommending an excellent book upon the subject by Professor Moulton of Chicago. One ought, however, to guard himself in a day when the spiritual has to fight hard for its place, against being so much fascinated by the form of speech as to neglect the contents of the message. This is to study the chasing of the golden cup, with its wreaths of passion flowers, and to forget the sacred essence which its holds; this is to be so taken by the binding of the book, with its fine tooling, as to leave its pages uncut. The literary appreciation of the Bible does not always imply its spiritual apprehension, but the Bible only yields its guerdon of blessing to the man who has heard therein the voice of

THE STANDPOINT OF THE BOOK 85

God, and obeyed the divine call. Artists scouring the coastline for a bit of fetching scenery, may be much taken by a fishing village nestling in the gorge between the cliffs, and fondly transfer to canvas the red roofs of the houses, and the security of the little harbour where the fishing boats are sheltered from the tumbling billows of the outer ocean. But it is only the fisherman who has made for that haven of refuge on a winter night when the storm was raging furiously and hungering for his life, and has heard the last angry wave beat helplessly upon the protecting rocks, as within his wife and children gave him welcome with thankful hearts, who can value at its full price the harbour which has been to him a hiding place from the wind and a covert from the tempest. Surely there is no person who can hear the promises of God's loving-kindness declared by the prophets without being vastly impressed by their majesty and beauty, but it is only the broken-hearted and conscience-stricken man laying hold of them in his despair, and casting himself as a last resource upon the pity and faithfulness of the Eternal, who understands their exceeding preciousness.

There is another theory regarding the purpose of the Bible which is very specious, and which has a great vogue in our own day. It was introduced by Spinoza the father of modern Pantheism in his " Tractatus theologico-politicus," in which he states the result of his investigation into Holy Scripture, and which has been popularized by that graceful man of letters Mr. Matthew Arnold in his " Literature and Dogma " and his " God and the Bible." Mr. Arnold wrote those two perfectly sincere and very interesting books to show that for long centuries people have misunderstood the object of the Bible. They have supposed in a quite pardonable ignorance that its chief aim was to teach men about God, but in fact it was intended to teach them about duty. Its substance is not dogma, it is ethics. The Bible is in short a handbook of conduct which differs from Aristotle's ethics or Plato's Republic or Seneca's Maxims, in being more strenuous in discipline and more gracious in spirit. Under

Mr. Arnold's superfine treatment, so complimentary to the Jewish writers, and so pitiful of common prejudices, God, who on first sight does seem very prominent and very real in the Bible, fades away and dissolves into "a power not ourselves, making for righteousness," and the miraculous is lightly dismissed as quite incredible and indeed too ridiculous. The Bible is presented to the modern mind, not as a book of religion but of practice, where the emphasis is laid, not on creed, but on conduct. Conduct is the motive of this literature, and therefore moderns who are sick of theology and who have no belief in the supernatural, but who cannot shake off their respect for the Bible, and who are quite convinced that, if it is to be well with a nation, the children must be trained in morals, propose to reduce it to a hand-book of good conduct, and hope that on this understanding it may be used by every person, those who believe in God, and those who do not. Mr. Arnold had an urbane style which is very pleasing, and he rendered service in calling attention to the ethical element in Holy

Scripture, and for that we should be grateful, but one cannot resist the conviction that in his appreciation of the Bible he had not quite risen to the occasion, and that he has failed to account for another element, and that is the spiritual. The Bible is very strong in teaching duty, but in this function it only exceeds by comparison, other books on morals; the Bible is most original when it is speaking of God, and here it is supreme and solitary. Its finest passages, say in the Psalms and in St. John's Gospel, are descriptions of what God is to man, and what man is to God; how He has sought for men, and how they have found Him. We should like to have those spiritual facts, and those personal experiences, this story of the inner life and these visions of the unseen explained. This is not conduct, though it is the spring of character; this is communion, the intercourse of the spirit of man with the spirit of God; man's soul returning to its birth. When I read the Twenty-third Psalm or the seventeenth chapter of St. John's Gospel, and I am told that the Bible was written in order to teach me to

THE STANDPOINT OF THE BOOK

live decently and to pay my debts, I am not satisfied. Those sublime passages are not accounted for, they still wait another exposition. If one visits an observatory, he is not satisfied until he has reached that lofty room open to the heavens, wherein the astronomers are studying the stars, and if he be told that this is only a rather more handsome and dignified dwelling-house, he has the suspicion of being played with. If the Bible be a mere guide to conduct, why was it built so high, why has it such an outlook?

We ought to distinguish between a book which is a spring of morality, and a book which is a guide to morals, and on this point the preacher should be very clear, and very careful. If he proposes to use the Bible as a companion of rules, he will both miss the intention of the Book, and lead his hearers astray. The principles of righteousness are certainly the same in all ages, and the Bible has been their most powerful exponent, laying them down with unequalled lucidity and authority, but the application of those principles to the circumstances of life changes in every age, and the understanding of those principles grows with the ages. Moses in the Ten Commandments, which is the summary of Old Testament ethics, and Jesus in the Sermon on the Mount, which is the enunciation of New Testament ethics, laid down principles, not rules, and for the most part it is the function of the preacher to lodge broad and clear conceptions of duty in the minds of his people, and to leave them to adjust those ideas to their particular environment. Was it not the chief mistake and also the hopeless futility of Pharisaism to meddle with the minute affairs of life, and to lay down what a man should do at every turn? It was not therefore an education for conscience, but a bondage of conscience; it did not bring men to their full stature by teaching them to face their own problems of duty and to settle them, it kept them in a state of childhood, by forbidding and commanding in every particular of daily life. Pharisaism, therefore, whether Jewish or Gentile, ancient or modern, which replaces the moral law by casuistry, and the enlightened judgment of

THE STANDPOINT OF THE BOOK 91

the individual by the confessional, creates a narrow character and mechanical morals. Freedom is the birthright of the soul, and it is by the discipline of life the soul finds itself. It were a poor business to be towed across the pathless ocean from this world to the next; by the will of God and for our good we must sail the ship ourselves, and steer our own course. It is the work of the Bible to show us the stars and instruct us how to take our reckoning.

One is tempted at this point to pause and to refer to a certain direction for living, which is often heard from the pulpit and a little while ago obtained the popular ear. Do you ask what ought one to do? and there seems no more clamant need. Ask another question: what would Jesus do? And you have an infallible answer. Would Jesus visit that place, read that book, associate with that person, undertake that work? If He would I may, if He would not I may not. It is such a simple solution of the practical perplexities of life, that one wonders why it was not discovered long ago, and why there should ever be any dividing of the roads. It ought to lift the shadow from the path of righteousness, it ought to bring all disciples of Christ to instant agreement on every point of duty. But as we all know this brief maxim of simple piety has not been an infallible or even applicable guide. And that for two reasons. The first is, that Jesus had a different work to do from us; He came to fulfill His high commission as the Redeemer of mankind and in its execution He discharged functions which are not ours, and endured sacrifices to which we are not called. He also had authority which is not given to us, and resources of grace which were His alone. Surely there is some difference between the action of the Captain of Salvation achieving the deliverance of the world upon the cross of Calvary, and that of a humble soldier carrying his cross amid the lowly affairs of life. The other reason is that the circumstances of Christ's life were different. What was becoming in the East, might not be in the West, what Jesus as a member of the Old Testament Church did, we may not be called upon to do in the new dispensation. The life of Jesus in Galilee both as a village workman, and as an itinerant prophet is not quite the same as that of a merchant or a barrister or a manufacturer or a clergyman of our day. What Jesus possessed He seems to have distributed among the poor, but if a rich man of to-day were to reduce his wealth to liquid cash and then fling it among the wastrels of a city, he would have taken the most successful means in his power of reducing self-respect, of fostering poverty, and of ministering to vice. You cannot imagine Jesus, if He had the means, buying a large farm and becoming a successful corn merchant, but if one of His disciples employed his resources to-day in building a manufactory in some country town, and giving employment to some hundreds of people upon fair terms, he would be rendering a practical service to the commonwealth, and be helping to build up men and women in habits of industry and in sound character. Jesus carefully refrained from interfering in the politics of His day, and never said one word against the oppression of the Roman yoke; He did not encourage His fellow countrymen to strike a blow for freedom and He cast the shield of His friendship over the hated tax gatherers. There were reasons for this attitude of the Master, and He was always justified in what He did, but if His disciples were to withdraw from all concern in the affairs of the state, and to be indifferent to the sacred cause of freedom, then politics would be left in the hands of the most selfish and corrupt section of the community, and nationality would perish beneath the hand of tyranny. This plausible suggestion, "What would Jesus do?" lends itself to discussions which become profane, and to situations which are childish, and this because it confounds the great principles of life with the minute details of conduct. Jesus has not told us what to do, for that were impossible, as every man has his own calling, and is set in his own circumstances, but Jesus has told us how to carry ourselves in the things we have to do, and He has put the heart within us to live becomingly, not by pedantic rules, but by an instinct

THE STANDPOINT OF THE BOOK

of nobility. Jesus is the supreme teacher of the Bible and He came not to forbid or to command, but to place the kingdom of God as a living force, and perpetual inspiration within the soul of man, and then, to leave him in freedom and in grace to fulfill himself.

Again, it is necessary for the preacher to remember that the Bible is not a book of theology, but that it has afforded the material for all the theologies. We ought to think clearly, and we may be helped in making this distinction by the difference between nature and science, which is the parallel to the difference between revelation and theology. Nature presents a vast field of phenomena, and it is the work of science to examine, to classify them, to find out the laws which govern them, and the effect which they produce. Science began very humbly and very weakly, and during the history of human knowledge, has been gradually extending her circle of light and embracing wider provinces in her kingdom. Science is ever making fresh discoveries and revising old theories, holding firmly what has been finally proved and keeping her mind open to what may yet be discovered. Science has had her disasters and her defeats; science has suffered and been put to death; science also has had her controversies, and has not been without her bigotries. But on the whole her march has been forward from twilight into sunshine, and science is honourably distinguished by self-denying labour, patient investigation, love of truth, and a belief in the order of the universe, and the unity of knowledge. However much science has learned, she believes that it is nothing to what will yet be conquered.

Theology in the same way has for her sphere the phenomena of revelation contained in Holy Scripture—the innumerable and marvellous experiences of the soul in its communion with God, and above all, the history of Jesus Christ, in which the religion of the Bible came to its height. The business of theology is to examine this wealth of spiritual facts, and to estimate their meaning, to consolidate them into doctrines which are simply generalizations and equivalent to laws in science, to discover also their practical application, and to bring them into relation with individual life. Theology is the science of religion, and has served a great purpose, as a handmaid to faith, and a nurse of religion. It is imperative that the preacher should have a working knowledge of theology, because unless he has an ordered system of thinking, his preaching will be invertebrate. Without a skeleton to support the fleshy body his sermons will be like a jellyfish, that most futile and helpless of creatures. Just however as a skeleton is concealed and does not appear in a perfect figure, so should a man's theology be covered by the flesh and blood of living humanity and practical religion.

The preacher, that is to say, ought to be a theologian, but not a professor of theology; he ought even to teach theology, but in such a manner that his congregation never know that they have received it. And in the study of theology, I suggest he should be guided by the following considerations: The first is, that he should base his theology upon the

Bible, and instead of building up doctrine with stones found in the quarry of philosophy, or taken from the ruins of ancient theological documents, that he should gather his facts from this comprehensive record of religion. Nothing is more dangerous in theology than laying down theories at the outset, of what God must do, or what God can do, and then making the facts of what He has done square with à priori dogmas. The return to the Bible is equivalent to the return to freedom, and the continual resort to this spring prevents theology from withering and dying. Nor should the preacher forget that theology is no more infallible than science, that it has made many mistakes, and may make many more, and that therefore while the theological explanation of regeneration or the Atonement is to be received with respect and to be used for the illumination of faith, no conclusion of theology is to be accepted as final, and none should be bound upon the acceptance of believing Christians. There is a wide gulf fixed between the allegiance to Christ and the acceptance of theology. As the Bible is better understood—and the Bible like nature is ever opening up fresh treasures—theological doctrines will have to be revised and readjusted; some may be discarded, and others will be created. The preacher also will not forget that theology is a progressive science, and that only upon those conditions can it exist. Some one has said that the concordance has been one of the worst enemies to theology, and if the writer meant the unscientific and unintelligent use of texts, he was speaking to the point. Under the old theory of an unprogressive revelation a text from Genesis had the same value as one from St. John's Gospel, and a reference to some local event in the Holy Land could be used to prove a principle of the spiritual life, with as much force as an argument of St. Paul. With our theory of spiritual evolution in our hand, and with our constant reference to the history of the time, we are able to assess texts at their right value, and to set them in their best light. We do not assume that Jacob knew as much of God as St. John; we do not place Job on the same level with the Epistle to the

Romans. Theology, therefore, has advanced from the conception of God, which made Him an arbitrary Eastern despot, who did whatsoever He pleased with His subjects, without regard to their merit or demerit, to that more convincing idea which makes Him the God and Father of the human family. There is an ancient town in Scotland which stands upon a rock that rises out of the plain. You can trace the history of the centuries in the architecture of the houses from the strong and dark fortress of the days of feud and blood, to the roomy and lightsome house of the modern time of peace and liberty, but all the houses rest upon the same rock, and for the most part were built with stone hewn from its bosom. So the Bible raises itself above the rich and fertile level of human literature, the immovable rock of God. Upon it all the theologies, Roman and Protestant, Calvinistic and Arminian are based, and out of its treasures their edifices have been gained. Some have grown obsolete and uninhabitable, some are modern and inviting. But each was justified in its turn and served its own purpose. And as on the height of that rock, there was a cathedral Church, in which men have worshipped through all the centuries, though under different rites, so let the preacher continually remind his people, and with the thought console their hearts in days of derision and confusion, that men of all schools and of all traditions within the Christian creed meet together in Christ Jesus their common Lord, and are sheltered beneath one roof, the wide-spread and kindly shield of the Fatherly love of God.

LECTURE III
THE HUMANITY OF THE BOOK

LECTURE III

THE HUMANITY OF THE BOOK

IF the inspiration of the Bible be of God, so that the Book may be justly called divine, its range is as wide as humanity. With its anchor cast within the veil, resting in the unseen and eternal, it compasses in its interest the circumference of human history. No religious literature, and no Christian preacher is as entirely and unreservedly human as the Bible, which embraces the universe of human incident and emotion. Within its pages is contained the story of the individual from youth to old age—Samuel in the Tabernacle and Simeon in the Temple; the story of the nation from its humble rise to its pitiable fall, from the bondage of Egypt to the siege of Jerusalem; the story also of the race from its emergence on the plane of life, on through its sin, its sorrow, its long martyrdom, its magnificent victories, till the glory of the nations passes in the vision of the poet through the gates of the city of gold. From the Eden of innocence in Genesis to the Garden of Holiness, in the book of Revelation, the Book marches. The whole comedy and tragedy of life are in this record; it is a more glorious Homer, a more enticing Scott. If its chief commandment of wisdom be "know God," and it has lifted the veil from the face of the Eternal, its second commandment is, "know thyself," and as in a mirror it shows every man his face. The secret motives which influence our actions, the hopes which nestle in the sacred place of the heart, the fears which shadow the pilgrim, as he makes his journey from this world to the next, the shining visions which float before the imagination in our highest moments, are all written in the words of this Book. Nowhere else has the possibility of human goodness or of human badness been so convincingly or profitably set forth. The ideals of heroic virtue, and the warnings of instructive wickedness are both found in its gallery. The double nature of man is described with such artless simplicity, and such incisive truthfulness, as never has been equalled in the subtlest fiction ; the riddle of our complex nature has been unravelled as it never has been in the profoundest philosophy, especially the glory of humanity, has been declared by the Incarnation, which reveals man as much as God. Against the despair of pessimists and the slander of satirists, is set the transfigured Person and radiant life of Jesus Christ, " white as no fuller on earth could white them," in whom all that the seers of the race had imagined was revealed, and all that the saints of the race desired was fulfilled. He is the typical man, to which the race is to rise ; as we look on Him, we know what man is to be and we measure his destiny.

Within the Bible every experience of life is touched in turn and the last word is said. The sweetest pastoral in literature is Ruth following Naomi for love's sake into a foreign land, and " fair among the fields of corn," gleaning after the reapers of Boaz. The saddest of tragedies is the fall of poor mad Saul, bravest and purest of the kings of Israel.

"Saul ye remember in glory—e'er error had bent
The broad brow from the daily communion;"

and the most touching elegy is the tribute of David to Saul, "Saul and Jonathan were lovely and pleasant in their lives, and in their death, they were not divided." There are three war songs which make the pulse beat faster, and would put courage in a coward, one was written by Burns, "Scots wha hae wi' Wallace bled." The second is "The Marseillaise," which rouses the French people to a frenzy, but the chief is that of Moses and Miriam, when he sang, "The Lord is a man of war, the Lord is His name," and Miriam with the women of Israel answered, "Sing ye to the Lord, for He hath triumphed gloriously, the horse and his rider hath He thrown into the sea." There was a day when Christians allowed themselves to despise St. Paul's Epistle to Philemon, the only private letter of the apostle's preserved, and to consider that its contents were trifling. The maxim of that day, as Bishop Lightfoot remarks, seemed to be "De minimis non curat evangelium." Of what account was the fate of a

THE HUMANITY OF THE BOOK 109

single insignificant slave, long since dead and gone, to those before whose eyes the battle of the creeds was still raging. Christians have grown more human since, and have passed further into the mind of Christ, and now they are agreed that even the letter of the younger Pliny, the very model of a Roman gentleman, when he asked a friend to show mercy to his freed men, is excelled in grace by the appeal of St. Paul for Onesimus. "We have here," writes Sabatier, " . . . only a few familiar lines, but so full of grace, of salt, of serious and trustful affection, that this short epistle gleams like a pearl of the most exquisite purity in the rich treasure of the New Testament." If it be one of the shortest portions in Holy Scripture, it is to be ever treasured by the Christian preacher, because it marks both the comprehensiveness and the minuteness of its humanity. Among the vices from which right-minded men turn with an instinct of disgust, and which they are moved to lash with indignant tongue, is hypocrisy, and the famous Philippics in which classical literature reached its highest note of scorn, fail before the irresistible scorching invective with which Jesus punished the Scribes and Pharisees before they accomplished their revenge. And if the virtue which wins our most cordial and unanimous applause is charity, its most finished and perfect eulogy was pronounced by the Apostle of the Gentiles in a passage which might have fallen from the lips of Jesus Himself.

If it is the Bible more than any poet or dramatist or essayist or novelist, which has released the strongest feelings of the human heart, and given them satisfying expression, it is also the Bible which has illustrated those situations in human experience in which life fulfills itself and character is declared. When we think of an unselfish and chivalrous friendship between two men of rich nature and high intention, our thoughts turn not to Damon and Pythias, the classical illustration of antiquity, but to David and Jonathan, and when the Prince of Israel said unto David, "Thou shalt be king over Israel, and I shall be next unto thee," the self-abnegation of friendship touched its zenith. Jacob was by nature a cunning and unscrupulous man, and it is not suggested that Rachel had the dignity of Sarah or the ability of Rebecca, but the most intimate love of husband and wife will never have a more tender instance than Jacob's serving seven years for Rachel, "And they seemed unto him, but a few days, for the love he had to her"; and at the thought of Rachel as he remembered her upon his death-bed, an old man full of years and sorrow, turning aside to mourn again; "Rachel died by me in the land of Canaan in the way, and I buried her there, in the way of Ephrath, the same is Bethlehem." We are taken to many kindly homes in the Bible stories, but to none do we go more pleasantly than to the house at Bethany, where Mary and Martha lived with their brother Lazarus, and had Jesus for their welcome and congenial guest. The peculiar bond which binds together a widowed mother and her only son has rescued from oblivion and made eternal the name of a Galilean village, for it was at Nain that Jesus had compassion on a stricken woman, and gave a son back to his mother. That passion, which is the travesty of love and the destruction of the family, has been the motive of many a novel and many a play, but has never been described and pilloried with such convincing proof and pitiless power as in the scandal of David and Bathsheba. History has produced a swarm of traitors, and there never has been any enterprise of the first order without its betrayer, but of all the men who have sold their cause, or their friend, none is to be compared with Judas Iscariot. When a rich man oppresses the poor, and tries to rob him of his little portion—a recurring and burning injustice of life,—one thinks in an instant of Ahab and Naboth. If a prophet receives the word of God, and understands its drift, and then for fear of man, or for the sake of gain perverts his message, and takes wages as the servant of unrighteousness, we class him with Balaam, who taught Balak to cast a stumbling-block before the children of Israel. There be many kinds of worldliness, but the most specious and dangerous is that which combines the profession of godliness with the greed of wealth, and this was the sin and the shame of Lot. Peter remains the type of men who lose their heads in the crisis of life and deny the Master whom they love, and Rebecca of clever and managing women who attain their ends by trickery and falsehood. While the world lasts, Abraham, who went out on his lonely journey as the pioneer of pure religion, will be the father of the faithful, and Moses, who stepped down from the side of a throne to take up the cause of a horde of slaves, will be the shining example of patriotism. When men of inspired vision and intellectual courage bid good-bye to the past, and go forward to possess the new land of truth into which the Lord is leading them, they will find their *leader* in St. Stephen. No minister of Christ will ever rise who will equal the enthusiasm, the humiliation, the sufferings, the magnanimity, the single-hearted devotion of St. Paul; and the mystics waiting for God in lonely places or in secluded studies, as those that watch for the morning, will ever envy him who in Patmos saw the heavens open and the Lamb leading His people to living fountains of water. Cain will remain forever the synonym for murderer; Methuselah from that dim antiquity for age; Ishmael, cast out by womanly injustice, and embittered in spirit, for the broken man; Joseph, beating down the insurrection of his youthful blood, and disentangling his garment from the hands of the temptress, for manly purity; Samson, triumphing with infinite humour over his enemies, during the days of his prosperity and in the days of his adversity pulling down a temple to be his tomb and monument, for strength. Jezebel in common speech will ever stand for a domineering and fierce-tempered woman; Abigail for gracious and timely service; Absalom with his undisciplined heart and his fair face, for filial impiety; Ahithophel with his far-seeing council for the shrewd adviser; Daniel with his sturdy loyalty to conviction, and his disregard of consequences, for courage; Herod stained by the massacre of the innocents, for cruelty; Gamaliel with his avoidance of haste and dislike of extremes, for an adroit ecclesiastic; Gallio with his elevation above religious squabbles, for judicial neutrality. If a society is formed to help poor women and to give other women the opportunity of service, it will likely be called after Dorcas of the Acts of the Apostles, and nearly every city has a hospital named after the good Samaritan of the gospels. When any one is richly dowered with sympathy and has grace poured into his lips, we call him after Barnabas the Son of Consolation, and Mary the mother of the Lord, has been through all the ages the ideal of womanly purity.

It is not only the preacher in the pulpit, but the speaker on the platform who is equipped with apt and telling images to seize the mind of his audience, and to plead his cause. He can draw from the gallery of life which is known to every one, whose faces are household portraits. The giant Goliath still falls before the sling and stone of youthful David, the trumpet is blown before the frowning fortress of some Jericho; Gideon's three hundred still win the victory of the single heart; the cave of Adullam gathers the refugees from regular authority into its shelter; Goshen is the image of a land of plenty, and Jordan stands for the river of Death. We call an unbeliever a Sadducee, and a formalist a Pharisee. A hypocrite is a whited sepulchre, an anxious person is a Martha, a doubter is a Thomas, and a guileless man is a Nathanael. The magnificent style of this book dignifies ordinary speech, and supplies felicitous expressions at every turn, so that men who hardly ever read the Bible, and others who have thrown off its authority, are still dependent upon it for phrases and illustrations. A popular orator advocating bi-metallism, describes his nation as crucified upon a cross of gold; an English statesman assailing the aristocracy, denounces them as those who toil not neither do they spin; a famous man of letters divided books into the sheep and the goats; prophets of woe warning their nation against the wrath to come, point them to the writing on the wall, and prudent persons standing aside from some doubtful cause, wash their hands of it, as Pilate did of Jesus. The Bible meets every emergency, and endows us with

THE HUMANITY OF THE BOOK 117

speech for every occasion—with proverbs which are the essence of experience, with commandments which are the compendium of morality, with prayers which release the desires of the heart, with promises which are the staff of life. The peasant who knows his Bible is richer in expression than the student of the classics, and the preacher with this book can awaken an echo within every hearer's heart. It might be possible outside the Bible, by ransacking literature in all ages and in all tongues, to get a corresponding gallery of types and situations, but it would be a strange place to the multitude, known only to a handful of literary archæologists. The preacher has been supplied with the most taking and most popular handbook to humanity.

The humanity of the Bible is as essential for its purpose as its divinity, and there is this double parallel between Holy Scripture which is the record of revelation, and Jesus Christ, who is the revelation itself, that the divine and human meet in both, and that until lately there was a tendency among believing people to undervalue the human side. If Jesus be the eternal Son of God, yet He was also the Son of Mary, a lad educated at Nazareth, a workman toiling at His craft, a prophet who was put to death by His nation; a man who was hungry and thirsty, who was tempted and persecuted, who was cast down and lifted up, who wore common garments, and lived in small homes. So if God has spoken with quite solitary authority through the Holy Scripture, the body of the Book is bone of our bone and flesh of our flesh. The story is of human life, as it fulfills itself in love affairs, in diplomatic negotiations, in mercantile transactions, in military campaigns, in the relations of husband and wife, parent and children, master and workman; as it is contained in ancient traditions, national poems, tribal histories, family chronicles; as it is stained by domestic intrigues, acts of hereditary revenge, violent outbursts of passion, hideous crimes of lust, as well as it is redeemed by instances of sacrifice, prayers of agonized souls, visions of saints, and achievements of heroes. The book is as human as

THE HUMANITY OF THE BOOK

Christ, and if it had not had this human nature, could no more have been for us men, a divine revelation than Christ without His human body, could have been a divine redemption. Through life God has revealed Himself. While there may be always speculation about the inspiration of the Bible, there is no doubt whatever that it is a historical revelation. While it is often repeated, "thus saith the Lord," and the word of the Lord did come to prophets whose ears He had opened, it might be still more truly and more widely stated "thus did the Lord," for it was by the Lord's doing, rather than His speaking that He made Himself known unto them who had eyes to see. The Bible, that is to say, moves, not in the region of philosophy, but in the region of history, not where men enquire into the being of God, but where they study the character of God. It is a book of common life, not a book of oracles. The end of revelation is ethical, not metaphysical. As has been said "the philosopher does not rule in Israel." Job may be called philosophy on a generous interpretation of the word, but Job is not philosophy in the Greek sense, and there is no other book which could be so described. St. Paul was a theologian in the most profound sense of the word, but he was not a theologian in the scholastic sense; he was writing from the depths of his own experience and with a pen dipped in blood and fire. The book is always moving, and the people are always acting; something is being done from the day when Samuel hewed Agag in pieces before the Lord, to the day when Jesus died upon the cross.

We should fix it in our minds on whom lies the commission of preaching the evangel, that it was only through history God could express Himself, lest we be caught in the snare of philosophy, and become theorists and not evangelists, weaving gossamer speculations about God, instead of boldly setting forth His actions. If the Messiah had only visited this earth as the angels did in the gospel story, appearing and disappearing before a few wrapt souls, then we had never known Him; if the eternal had spoken from

THE HUMANITY OF THE BOOK

an open heaven to one or two elect men, such as Abraham and Moses, then Israel had never come to call Him their Holy One. It is only through the consciousness of men that God can make Himself known, an ever brightening and more pervading presence in life. As the years come and go, God makes His arm bare in times of trouble and comforts in times of sorrow, and guides in times of darkness. If He be real to the fathers, He becomes more living to the children, till saints, even in the midst of this shadow and surrounded with the mystery of life, can cry, "Why art thou cast down, O my soul, and why art thou disquieted within me? Hope in God for I shall yet praise Him, who is the health of my countenance, and my God."

Until the memory of living men, Christian preachers were afraid to insist upon the humanity of Jesus, lest they should be supposed to deny His divinity, and so in many cases they had fallen over into the opposite heresy; so the human element in scripture was spiritualized out of existence. As fields of flowers are swept and crushed and mixed with foreign material and distilled into an essence, so the rich provinces of human life in Holy Scripture were robbed of all their dramatic incidents that they might yield the doctrines of technical theology. The love and hate, the striving and ambition, the despair and victory, the laughter and the tears of men and women, passed in to this remorseless machinery, and came forth Election or Justification, the Covenant of works or the Covenant of Grace. When you read a Dutch theologian like Witsius, or a Puritan like Owen, you wonder how men could have had the Bible in their hands all their days and studied it with honest, prayerful hearts, and yet never have detected the method of revelation or felt the breath of its common humanity upon their faces. We ought to be thankful that to-day a more real and comprehensive view of the Incarnation has taken hold of the Christian mind, that we believe in the Incarnation not only as a fact but also as a force, that Christ was not only actually born into the race, but that He lived so many years in the Holy Land, as a man lives to-day in America or England, and that He is still living and proving His presence in the direction and elevation of human life. He is within and not outside humanity, and in the same way we ought to hold that God is inside and not outside life, an immanent not transcendental deity.

With the humanity of the Bible as a spirit in his heart, the preacher should be able to preach a living God, as He was not preached when that humanity was denied. It is nothing short of unbelief to hold that the action of God is confined within the centuries which are embraced in the Bible record, and that if we desire to find God we must go to Palestine instead of America. We should be firmly convinced that the Eternal who made Himself known to the patriarchs in their tents, and the prophets in Jerusalem, is as near to-day to shepherds in their glens and merchants amid the turmoil of great cities. It were disheartening to think that God who spake to Abraham does not speak to men today, or that He spoke to the Jews after a nearer and more friendly fashion than to our generation. That He did make Himself known to the Fathers is beyond question, but that He made Himself far more clearly known by His Son is quite as certain and therefore we may boldly say that in the dispensation of Christ at the right hand of God, God is still more active in human history, still more visible to human souls. When we have firmly grasped the idea of historical revelation, and our minds are cleansed from the idea that God is a provincial or temporal deity, we shall be the more ready to recognize Him in the present time and to put our trust in Him as a God near and not far off. And <u>the recognition of God is the transfiguration of life</u>, both on the larger historical and on the lesser individual scale. If Bible history is lit by the fires of Sodom and Gomorrah, and the horrors of the siege of Jerusalem, God also wrought terrible works of judgment, in the catastrophies of the Roman Empire and the French Revolution. If God was the deliverer of the oppressed and the hope of those that put their trust in Him in the days of Israel, surely His right arm succoured the

Protestants of the low country in their resistance of Philip and his Spaniards and opened up a way for the Puritans in this land and built them into a strong people. If the converts of St. Paul were to be numbered by hundreds, the converts of Wesley were to be reckoned by thousands, and if St. Luke wrote the first romance of missions, surely it has been continued with chapters quite as convincing and fascinating in the lives of St. Francis Xavier, David Brainerd, Father Damien, and David Livingstone. The answers to prayer in Holy Scripture can be paralleled in the lives of saints who have lived centuries after the canon was closed and thousands of miles away from the land of sacred wonder. While the preacher speaks he is thrown into relief against a historic background which is full of God, he stands in the presence of the Eternal, who is the God and Father of our Lord Jesus Christ, and is doing yet more abundantly and revealing Himself yet more clearly than in the ages of patriarchs, prophets, or apostles.

The Bible in this historical setting becomes

not an ancient but a modern book; it is contemporaneous, and we are at liberty to be indifferent as to its dates, because we can place it in many periods. Books of the Bible which had almost passed into oblivion, suddenly glow with light, because they describe a similar situation, and prophesy a similar deliverance. The Puritans drew strength from the iron age of the Judges, and went into battle and died for the freedom of their nation to the trumpet call of the sword of the Lord and Gideon. The fiery letter which St. Paul wrote to the Galatians and in which he asserted the supremacy of grace over works, and of the cross over ritual—the magna charta of the human soul—inspired Martin Luther and was the spring of the Reformation. Social reformers raging against the luxury and tyranny of the rich, and full of pity and sympathy for the poor, striving and praying for their Utopia have found their leaders in the Hebrew prophets, while the martyrs, hiding in dens and caves of the earth, or dying in the blood-stained arena, have been lifted above their suffering and assured of their victory by the vision of the Apocalypse. The Bible situations are endlessly repeated because the Book is not the detached achievement of a scholar's study, but the harvest of centuries of human life. If the nation finds God in its public life, should not the individual find Him in his private life, and ought not the preacher to insist more constantly and more practically, that if we are to know God it must be through life? If the Eternal made Himself known in the past through history, will He not make Himself known in the present through biography? Whether is it more in keeping with the Bible to send the child to learn of God in a catechism or in its own home; whether is God more likely to be real to the child when His nature is stated in the abstract terms of theology or by the analogy of his father and mother? Is it not also the lesson of the Bible, that the knowledge of God is dependent, not upon reasoning, but upon obedience, and that no speculation will ever bring us so near God, as action? Was it not by doing God's will that man came to know Him in the Bible, and was it not because Israel at its best in its saints and prophets loved and did righteousness, that in the clean mirror of their souls, God was reflected, as on the quiet surface of a lake the eternal mountains shape themselves? Amid the inevitable mystery of life and the vexing questions which agitate the intellect, men should be reminded that light always arises to the righteous, that wherever a man is bravely doing his duty, he is in the way of life everlasting, and must sooner or later come into the conscious fellowship of God. To say that the Bible is intended to teach nothing but conduct and that it presents no person, is to come short of facts; but to say that conduct is a road to faith and that the righteous man ascendeth to the Hill of God is one of the most profound facts of Bible life.

While the preacher has reason for insisting that the Bible as a whole is contemporaneous because it is historical, which is only another way of stating that humanity is the same in all climes and in all ages, he should frankly admit, or rather he is bound to point out, that upon the principle of evolution certain parts of the Bible are obsolete. The worship of the Jews for instance has now no authority for the Christian Church, and time need not be wasted in studying its sacrifices, any further than understanding the references of some New Testament writers when they state the work of Christ in altar terms. It is amazing to remember the time that was given by worthy divines of the past to the processes of sacrifice laid down in the books of Moses, when the same time could have been spent upon the life of Christ, and the careful exposition of Jewish ritual, when the same care might have been bestowed on the exposition of Jesus' words. The chronicles of the Jews and their ritual together with many of their social regulations may be laid aside, for they possess now nothing but an antiquarian interest. With those remains of the past in the limbo of superseded ideas may be placed the rude conception of God in the earlier Scriptures. Surely it is, to say the least, untimely that the Christian preacher should be representing God, as a jealous and revengeful deity, who requires to be reconciled by blood before He will show mercy, and who is provoked to anger if any mother should forget Him for the moment in devotion to her child. When the preacher speaks as if God required to be reconciled to His children, he is standing on the Old Testament but he is contradicting the New, and when he teaches that some loved one is taken away in order that the affection given to the wife or child, should be monopolized by Him, he has surely not heard of our Heavenly Father. Surely Jesus' teaching counts for something, and if He superseded the law of Moses, has He not also spiritualized the God of Moses? If I am not bound to-day to offer bulls and goats because the Jews offered them in Old Testament days, neither am I bound to believe in a suspicious and grasping deity, such as they feared in the days of their childhood. Jesus Himself laid down the principle that religious ideas are to be tried by human experience and according to the religious consciousness must therefore be the conception of God. It follows that Isaiah

THE HUMANITY OF THE BOOK 131

would have a more gracious consciousness than Moses and that the idea of God in the minds of Christian people on whom the spirit of Jesus has been playing, should not only be clearer but sweeter than that of Old Testament religion. If considerable portions of the Old Testament, both legal and spiritual have not been superseded by the teaching of Jesus, so that they are no longer to be quoted or preached as truth, then Christ has come in vain and there has been no advance from the patriarchs to the Messiah.

While it is necessary to distinguish between the temporary element in the Old Testament, which has no force to-day, and the eternal, which is as true and binding to-day as ever, let us be careful in making this distinction, and not, in laying aside what has served its day, part with any real treasure. There are certain books of the Old Testament which have fallen into disrepute and into disuse for various reasons, but which ought to be studied afresh with the aid of criticism and from the standpoint of humanity. They have one way or other been sold into captivity, and ought to be redeemed. One I frankly admit it is difficult to appreciate from the New Testament standpoint, because it appears to have no spiritual message. Should any Christian be asked what book of the Old Testament he would omit, I take it he would answer the book of Esther. He would be expressing not only a Christian instinct, but also confirming a Jewish objection. The rabbis had great difficulties about its inspiration because it was so secular, without a mention of the name of God; and so foreign, mentioning the King of Persia a hundred and eighty-seven times. There is no doubt, however, it was included in the Jewish canon when the latter was closed at the council of Jamnia in the first century, and it became afterwards extremely popular with the Jewish people. It is the most unchristian book in the Old Testament, and it is also the least religious by any standard; but Esther justified its place in the canon by its spirit of intense and self-sacrificing patriotism. By her beauty, according to the story, which can hardly be looked on as historical, and by her courage as well as by her womanly tact, she saved her people from a cruel massacre during the Persian captivity; and to commemorate this deliverance the feast of Purim was instituted, which is the celebration of nationality. When theological ingenuity endeavours to read Christian truth into this book, it turns Scripture into a cryptogram, and lays an unnecessary burden upon the religious mind, but it does not follow that the book with all its defects and all its offenses has not made its contribution to human history. It is a vindication of nationality, that every people, however weak and unfortunate, has a right to live; it is a condemnation of wanton cruelty, that a strong man should order a massacre for reasons of personal revenge. It is an incentive to patriotism, teaching that people of one blood should recognize their common tie, and that in a nation rich and poor should stand together for their rights; and it is a eulogy on womanly courage, for here was a young queen who was willing to risk her place and her life in the interests of her people. No doubt she used her influence for vengeance upon the chief enemy of her people and those who attacked them, but even here patriotism, though bloodthirsty, was not mercenary, for the Jews, if they slew, did not plunder. The book sustained the Jews in after ages amid their unmitigated and unmerited sufferings, and, rightly read, may still infuse the iron of patriotism into the veins of a nation either oppressed by force or enervated by luxury. It is a book which requires to be dated "B. C.," and then to be cleansed by the spirit of Christ; but when it is first related to its period, and then elevated above it, it remains a call both to national and civic patriotism, and a condemnation of those who, if it go well with themselves and their own interests, have no care for the mass of the people from whom they sprang and whose blood they share.

The second of the unredeemed books is the prophecy of Jonah, and here one is on much surer ground, and has a more convincing case. Nothing is easier of course for an outsider to the Bible and to faith than to ridicule this book, and believers have too much played into his hands. Because the story is so dramatic and because the dramatic device is somewhat rude and simple; because many good people have refused to see the dramatic element and have closed their eyes to the hopeless absurdity of its reality, the book has been made a thing for laughter. The preacher, therefore, must bend his back to brush the scorn from off this fine work of Jewish literature, and seizing its spiritual intention, vindicate its execution. The central figure is Jonah, who was a prophet in the reign of Jeroboam II, and whose preaching at Nineveh was no doubt a historical fact, but the incidents of this book are not known to history, and it must have been written at a far later date than the life of Jonah. It was a book of the post-exilic period when the attitude of the Jews to the Gentiles was one of sullen resentment and acrid bigotry. This book is an exposition of the all embracing love of God, to whom Nineveh was as dear as Jerusalem, and a satire on the narrowness of Jewish religion which would monopolize God and count every man of Gentile blood an outcast. When Jonah refuses to go with the gospel of divine mercy to Nineveh, and when he is jealous of the conversion of the Ninevites, he represents the worst spirit of Jewish religion; and when the heathen seamen show their good spirit on board the vessel, and the Ninevites repent at the word of the Lord, the piety which may exist outside the line of Jewish revelation is convincingly suggestive. It may be granted that the whale is a somewhat inartistic expedient, but the rest of the book is most artistically arranged, and is charged with the highest spiritual meaning. If only a Philistine would laugh at the parable of Andromeda and the Sea Monster, which has been so often painted, why should any one mock at the device of the Jewish writer? Can there be found anywhere a more telling exposure of national exclusiveness, or a more engaging assertion of the love of God towards all men, and towards the very beasts of the field, than in the book which declares that if a man has pity for the gourd, "for the which thou hast not laboured neither madest it grow, which came up in a night and perished in a night," surely the Creator and Father of all men would "spare Nineveh that great city, wherein are more than six score thousand persons that cannot discern between their right hand and their left hand, and also much cattle." This gracious and genial book was as a root out of a dry ground, and so comprehensive is its charity, and so gracious its view of God, that it is a question whether the Christian Church with all her advantages in the dispensation of the Holy Ghost holds as firmly, and declares as unreservedly the universal Fatherhood of God, and the brotherhood of man. It is the irenicon of the Old Testament.

The Song of Songs is one of the most exquisite books in Holy Scripture, and came from the finest period of Hebrew literature, but the Jewish scholars themselves were perplexed by its theme, and in the early Christian centuries there were doubts about its canonicity. It was only saved from exclusion, and included in the Scriptures, first possibly because its authorship was ascribed to Solomon, and certainly because it received an allegorical meaning. Had it been regarded as a love drama, it would certainly have been excluded when the canon was finally concluded, and in modern days it would never have been so much in favour with pious people. But it was looked upon as a parable of the fellowship between the Church and Christ, and at the Sacrament addresses based on its warmest passages were delivered with unction and effect. Its spiritual interpretation has been a triumph of mysticism, in which the most erotic language has been charged not only with religious experiences, but even with elaborate doctrine. The idea that this book could have had love as its original motive and be a poem on the chief passion of life, would have been repudiated in days when the humanity of the Bible was not only ignored, but denied. With the return to a more real and historical view of the Bible, the Christian mind is prepared for a more literal and human reading of the Song of Songs. Whoever was its author, it could not be Solomon, and it is far more likely that the poem was a powerful and skillful protest against the immorality of that luxurious monarch and his corrupt court. It is indeed a romance such as effects the popular mind in every age, and whose theme has never been treated with such beauty. Besides the chorus, which is supplied by the ladies of the court, the persons are the king, a magnificent and dissolute monarch, the heroine, a beautiful and simple country girl, and her lover a young and honest shepherd. During some royal journey through the provinces, the King's eye falls upon this rustic maiden, and after his habit he desires to add her to his harem. She is brought to Jerusalem, and is given a place in the palace, but her heart remains true to her shepherd lover, and in her dreams she recalls their meeting in the fields, and seeks for him through the streets of the city. She rejects the advances of the King, and declares her longing to be again with her betrothed; finally she returns in safety, and the poet concludes with a lovely description of the meeting between the two lovers, and the contempt which she pours upon the addresses of Solomon and all his riches. The poem reaches its height in the eulogy of pure and unworldly love : "Set me as a seal upon thine heart, as a seal upon thine arm, for love is strong as death. . . . Many waters cannot quench love, neither can the floods drown it. . . . Solomon hath a vineyard at Baalhamon ; he let out the vineyard unto keepers ; every one for the fruit thereof was to bring a thousand pieces of silver. My vineyard which is mine is before me ; . . . make haste my beloved and be thou like to a roe or a young hart upon the mountains of spices."

Does it not invest the Bible with a fresh interest, that this pure and fascinating love idyll should be included in its compass and that the chief book of humanity should place the crown upon simple and unworldly love, and pay this noble tribute to the country maiden who resisted the unholy advances of magnificent Solomon. Transfer the scene for instance to England and the seventeenth century ; replace Solomon by Charles II and the Shulamite by some English country girl ; imagine her enveigled to Whitehall and assailed by the blandishments of that gay court, and then invulnerable against all Charles's appeals and faithful to her rustic lover, returning in triumph to her home amid the greenery and oak trees of some English county. If any one in those days had been given the spiritual genius to make this powerful and graceful protest against the most licentious king and the most degraded court in English history, how we should have cherished and admired his poem, and how generations to come would have counted it the classic love piece of our tongue! What neither English literature nor any other has afforded is given by the Song of Songs in perfect and unapproachable beauty.

The fourth book of Old Testament Scripture which illustrates the wide humanity of the Bible is Ecclesiastes, and no one can blame the Jewish doctors for hesitating about the inclusion of this book. The Song of Songs may be allegorized into religion, but no ingenuity can spiritualize the Preacher. It is the dreariest book in the whole Bible, and touched throughout by the spirit of pessimism. Certainly it was not written by Solomon or any other king, for the standpoint is that of the people who are suffering and helpless under misgovernment, and who are hopeless of either reform or justice. The writer himself seems to have been wronged by society and to have lost faith in every one, rulers and people, men and women together. Everything is out of joint, and his only consolation is a cold and hesitating faith in the moral order of the world. It is indeed as nearly as possible the utterance of one who has despaired of human society and has only the faintest hope in God. He is the agnostic of the Bible, and it is one of the most convincing evidences of the range of Holy Scripture that room is found in it, "for the sigh of defeated hopes, for the gloom of the soul, vanquished by the sense of the anomalies and mysteries of human life." If there be not room in the Christian creed or in the Christian Church for a man with this irreducible minimum of faith, he is made welcome in the Bible, and the complaint of his soul expressed. For he also is a son of God.

The Bible, in short, reaches from the depths of human experience where the mist is lying heavy upon the valley to the heights where the soul lives in the shining of God's face, and each man can find his own level in the Book. The lad whose blood is dancing and who loves the excitement of life, will be vastly taken with the homeric conflicts of Hebrew champions, with Samson and his foxes, with David and Goliath ; the business man shrewd and worldly wise, will find in Proverbs the experience of life, as in an essence ; the seeker after God will have prayers laid to his hands in the Psalms, and the religious soul will be satisfied with St. Luke's Gospel, the most beautiful book in all the world. If you turn over the pages of a private Bible you can almost tell the age of its owner, and if he be "stepping westward" and the light of the setting sun be on his face, you will find that the fourteenth chapter of St. John's Gospel has been worn thin. It has indeed become but a slight veil, which some day will disappear, and the faithful Christian who has followed the Lord through many experiences, both of light and shadow, will at last stand face to face with Him, whom not having seen he loves.

LECTURE IV

THE AUTHORITY OF THE BOOK

LECTURE IV

THE AUTHORITY OF THE BOOK

IF it be granted that criticism has increased our knowledge of the Bible, has it not diminished its authority, so that a preacher cannot use the book with the same confidence as in past days, nor expect its words to have the same hold on the allegiance of his people? According to the old idea of the Book it came directly from God, through the hands of writers who were simply its penmen, and were guided so absolutely by the Holy Spirit, that they could not commit any error in facts or in doctrine. They simply transmitted the mind of the Eternal to His creatures. Possibly a guarded use of accommodation might be allowed, but progression in revelation was unknown. The Book was therefore of equal authority from its first volume to its last, and in all its parts. If a word was quoted, unless it had been uttered by an enemy of God in Bible history or had the most obvious local reference, it was an end to controversy, for it was the intervention of God. Any one in perplexity would turn to the Scriptures for guidance, and any text spoken to his case would be accepted as in old days men received the oracles of Delphi, and it was not unusual for pious people of a simple mind to allow the Bible to open and then to seek advice from the first passage which caught their eye, which was practically a casting of lots. Promises were then ministered to souls in distress, and they were exhorted to put their trust in the word, as a communication made to them from the very lips of God. If people within the province of faith differed in those days, it was not about the validity of any single word, it was only about its interpretation. The evidence was perfectly undeniable, the only question was, when it was all arranged and summed up, about its balance. The Arminian would not endeavour to escape the force of any quotation from the Old Testament Scriptures, in the interests of the most absolute and pitiless predestination; he would content himself by bringing forward other texts to colour and qualify. A single incident in Jewish history would justify the most amazing action in modern times, so that Puritans perpetrating the Irish massacres found their defense in the doings of the Judges, and the imagery of Hebrew seers was accepted to the letter, so that in the days of the Commonwealth veteran soldiers, tried in many fights, were going about to establish the Fifth Monarchy. To-day there are excellent people who use the Bible to calculate the end of the world, and who by a stringent use of prophetic rhetoric, expect to see Jerusalem again the Holy City and the sacrifices once more offered in the temple. With this view of the Bible, men could be silenced, comforted, enlightened, rebuked, by a single phrase chosen almost at will, from its rich and varied story. The preacher could speak with boldness, for what he said was not of man but of God, and the pastor could console with confidence, for he carried with him, and applied to the heart in trouble, the very grace of God.

Can this impressive principle of authority be maintained under the modern idea of the construction of the Bible? If the Book is a long and comprehensive literature, extending over many centuries and marking many stages of progress, can it lend itself to the same treatment, and be as confidently handled? Will it not be necessary to consider the date of any passage which is to be used, and the character of the man through whom it was given; will not the Scriptures have to be analyzed historically and arranged spiritually; will not the religious value of each part have to be fixed, and the comparative value of the various parts calculated? How shall we know whether what is said in the Old Testament has been abolished in the New, and what force to attach to a word put in the mouth of a patriarch compared with the utterance of a prophet? If the Apostles are superior to the prophets, what function has prophecy, and if Jesus be the supreme teacher in the Bible, what place is there for His servants? Is the preacher to discuss the critical position of every passage before he

THE AUTHORITY OF THE BOOK 151

uses it, which would be intolerable pedantry, and the destruction of the pulpit, or is he to use every part of the Bible as if criticism had never existed, with the result that his voice have a note of insecurity, and reading men in his Church dismiss his evidence as irrelevant? Is the only course open to him to claim no divine authority for the Bible, but only to treat it as one of the supreme books of religion, and its utterances as suggestions towards the religious life? The preacher then ceases to be the ambassador of God and becomes a lecturer on religion, or an ethical teacher. This is a very serious question for the minister, and one is afraid that in some quarters criticism has weakened the power of the pulpit, and by depriving the preacher of an infallible book has left him intellectually and spiritually helpless. If this were the inevitable effect of criticism, then the increase of knowledge would be a poor compensation for the loss of power, and one would regard with dismay a method of study which enriched us with secondary information about the Bible, and silenced the voice of God through its length and breadth.

We ought to face this question and to think it out clearly. First of all let us ask ourselves how those Scriptures came to be regarded as the word of God. They are only a portion of many writings both in the days of the Old Testament and of the New. Yet they have been elected, and the Apocrypha of the Old Testament and the Apocryphal Gospels of the New have been rejected. No doubt there has been difficulty because of the inclusion of, say, Ecclesiastes and of St. James' Epistle, but long ago the Canon was completed and has remained unchanged. There are moments when one would be willing to exchange the Book of Esther, for, say, the Wisdom of Sirach, and to give up the Epistle of St. Jude for the Imitation of Christ or the Pilgrim's Progress. But those are only passing impulses, for when one looks first at the Holy Scriptures as a whole and next at the other books he will certainly conclude that the selection has been justified, and that the Bible stands apart and

THE AUTHORITY OF THE BOOK

supreme. But who made the selection? Was this done by a supernatural method, the voice of an oracle or a declaration by Jesus, and His Apostles? The Canon was fixed by the Church, by Jews for the Old Testament, by Christians for the New. In other words by a body of fallible men. When it is said that the Church created the Canon, and that the Church is the guardian of the Bible it should be remembered that the Church did not assign their spiritual value to the books, but that their spiritual value forced them upon the Church, and that if the Church has the duty of expounding the Bible, then the book itself is immortal.

If the Bible is stamped with this hallmark of the Canon by the Church, it is because every one knows the Bible to be gold, and not because the Church can make it gold. The Bible is presented, therefore, if you look into the matter, not by the authority of the Church but by its own authority, and claims the acceptance of the human soul, not because the Church bears witness to its excellence, but because it bears witness to itself. The Spirit of God within its revelation speaks to the spirit of God within a man's heart. The authority of the Bible is therefore spiritual in the appeal which as a whole it makes to the intellect and to the conscience.

It is a fourth rate kind of unbelief which denies the spirituality of the Bible, or its high place in the province of religion, but there is a tendency in other and better quarters to depreciate the authority of the Bible in comparison with other books, or rather to deny its supremacy by pointing out that it is only one out of many felicitous contributions to the religious spirit. Why make so much of the Bible as a book of morals, as an ideal of character, as a conception of God, as a message to the soul, as a vindication of charity, when those great services have been splendidly discharged by books which are quite independent of the Hebrew Revelation? Can any words describe the way of righteousness more perfectly than the hymn of the stoic Cleanthes,

" Lead me, O Zeus, and thou O Destiny,
The way that I am bid by you to go:
To follow I am ready. If I choose not,
I make myself a wretch, and still must follow."

Which has been admirably translated into parallel Christian terms by the late Bishop Stubbs the historian.

" Lead me, Almighty Father, Spirit, Son;
Whither Thou wilt I follow, no delay;
My work is Thine, and even had I none,
Grudging obedience still I will obey;
Faint-hearted, fearful, doubtful if I be,
Gladly or sadly I will follow Thee.
Into the land of righteousness I go,
The footsteps thither Thine and not my own;
Jesus, Thyself the way alone I know,
Thy will be mine for other have I none;
Unprofitable servant tho' I be,
Gladly or sadly let me follow Thee."

Has not Plato described in terms which echo the fifty-third verse of Isaiah, the righteous man who shall be unjustly accused and make no complaint and suffer meekly, for the good of the people? Did not the great Mogul Emperor Akbar embrace within his charity all men who under any creed or by any worship sought after God, so that in every temple he found God's servants and in every prayer heard their cry? Did not Marcus Aurelius in his "Thoughts" which Renan declared to be "the most human of all books," and "the Gospel that will never grow old," give a noble example of the fellowship of the soul with God, and that devotion to the highest ends which surely constitute life everlasting? In the third millennium B. C. a code of laws was enacted by a King of Babylonia which is not unworthy of Moses, and must have profoundly affected Hebrew tradition. The Egyptian theology had a doctrine of the Trinity and the "Book of the Dead" not only affirms the immortality of the soul but lays down in picturesque terms the salutary doctrine of rewards and punishments. Confucius laid the foundations of family morality for China, and the doctrine of the Incarnation is embedded in the great religion of the East.

There was a day when Christian people disliked the idea of any revelation either of faith or morals outside the Bible, and when missionaries did not think it necessary to find the points of contact between the Christian religion, and the faiths of the nations to which they were sent. There is still an idea that if a great Christian doctrine were to be found in its essence outside the Bible, that in some fashion its reality has been denied, and that, if there were in human minds the seed of Christianity already sown, Christianity therefore must be a fond invention. It was held, if it was not asserted, that the divinity of Christianity rested upon the fact that it was something no one could have anticipated or imagined, and that it had no relation to human thought or human experience. Ought we not rather to think that if the Bible be the supreme knowledge of God it will declare in their clearest and most engaging forms those ideas of the Eternal after which men have been feeling for ages, and that it will be the fulfillment of many hopes? Is it not reasonable to believe that God did not forget the nations though He spoke most plainly to the Hebrew people, and that though Christ came according to the flesh of the house of David, yet He was the light which lighteth every man that cometh into the world? Has not the Bible revelation both of God and of conduct been confirmed, if it can be shown that already it was dimly diffused among the prophets of many people, and that Plato and Aurelius have also carried the message of God? Would the Bible be more credible if it were quite detached from human life; is it not more entirely human when its roots are found to be struck in the reason and conscience of humanity? A Christian minister may do worse than have on a shelf near his hand the Saints and Seers of the nations, for he will obtain a wider view of the Fatherhood of God, and build himself up in a braver hope regarding the future of his race.

This recognition of the larger grace of God need not impinge upon the unique authority of Holy Scripture, for the Bible in comparison with other books is unapproachable, if the comparison be wisely and justly made. No doubt nobler utterances can be found in Plato than in the earlier Old Testament Scriptures: I will not even say that Epictetus is on every occasion hopelessly out-distanced by St. Paul; but there can be no question that when you compare the prophets of the Gentile succession with those of the Hebrew line, that the Bible has a lonely place. The Gospel of St. John raises its head high above every other conception of God and of the religious life, and if it were possible, as some have said, to find elsewhere many of the finest sayings in the Sermon on the Mount, was it not Jesus who took them like rough ore, stamped them with His own Image and sent them into circulation. This Book has not only revealed ideals of character, it has created the reality of that which it revealed. With other books the morality has been maxims; in this book it has been acts. In other books the idea of God has been a dim imagination, in this book a practical revelation.

The solitary position of the Bible may also be realized if one considers its catholicity, and compares it in the matter of breadth with other books of the Christian religion. Most ministers have on their table a bracket of books of devotion, drawn from Christian springs and full of the Christian spirit. No one can over-estimate the service to the Christian life rendered by such works as Law's "Serious Call," Bunyan's "Pilgrim's Progress," Baxter's "Saint's Rest," à Kempis' "Imitation of Christ," Rutherford's "Letters," and Taylor's "Holy Living and Dying." They are all admirable, but they are all provincial. There are people who cannot read Rutherford, because he is so sensuous in his imagery, and others who object to à Kempis because he is so ascetical. Law is thought by some not to be Evangelical, and Taylor to be too rhetorical. But the people who will argue over those manuals of piety and come to no agreement because of different heredity and different tastes, will find themselves at home within Holy Scripture. A Presbyterian divine declares "The haughty contempt of that book (Rutherford's "Letters") in the heart of many will be ground of condemnation, when the Lord cometh to make inquisition after such things," and no doubt other books would be

THE AUTHORITY OF THE BOOK 161

made a standard of personal piety. But we may be perfectly certain it will not be by any provincial standard that we shall be judged, but by the large and broad rule of Holy Scripture, wherein every man findeth what he desires, and is satisfied. The Bible is supreme, not only because it has exceeded all other books both in its vision, and in its dynamic together, but because it has gathered into itself all the excellency which has been diffused throughout the prophecy of many nations.

As the Bible, however, in distinction from other books of religion is a prolonged literature, with an immense mass of detail, one may not claim that the book as a whole and in all its parts is authoritative, and therefore the minister should clearly lay down what is the authoritative element in Holy Scripture. Upon first sight this may seem a difficult and irreverent task. "Do you propose," a conservative critic will ask, "to go through the Bible with a black lead-pencil and to erase such passages as you may not think binding on the soul, as if you were a censor checking literature at the frontier of religion? What right have you to cut up the Bible after this fashion; upon what principle of discrimination will you go? What guarantee of certainty have you that you will take the right and leave the wrong? Will this mangled corpse be worth possessing when you have finished your dissecting?" This objection would be very telling, and indeed unanswerable, if one were simply to pick and choose throughout Holy Scripture according to his fancy, but this is not what one is proposing. And in turn one may ask the question of his critic: when he is preaching for the guidance of human souls, or when he is comforting his people in distress, does he take indifferently a Chronicle of names, or the story of a battle, or the murder of a king, or the complaint of Ecclesiastes? Does he not rather turn to one of those beautiful and gracious passages which in one age and another declare the loving-kindness and tender-mercy of God, or one of those irresistible invitations wherein Christ gathers human souls into His love, as a hen gathereth her

THE AUTHORITY OF THE BOOK 163

chickens under her wings? Of course he does, and however extreme may be his theory of the absolute infallibility and equal authority of all portions of Holy Scripture, he will let that theory go by the board when he is bringing the Bible to bear upon the wants of the human soul. What does this mean, this preference of a comfortable word of Christ to the war-like utterance of a Hebrew judge, this elevation of the eighth chapter of the Epistle to the Romans over the regulations of Leviticus, but that God's voice does sound more clearly and more kindly in some portions of Scripture than in others? We do not erase Scriptures, but we elevate Scriptures; we do not refuse to hear any voice that speaks, but we can recognize the voice of our Father, and when it sounds in our ears, whether in the Old Testament or the New, we give it welcome. That is the heart of the Bible, and when that Voice speaks the soul is bound to hear.

We must in short distinguish between the Book and its message, between the record and the revelation, a distinction which is made in the Shorter Catechism with point and lucidity. Q. "What rule hath God given to direct us how we may glorify and enjoy Him?" A. "The word of God which is contained IN the Scriptures of the Old and New Testaments, is the only rule to direct us how we may glorify and enjoy Him." The gospel, to use its royal name for the message of God, is the soul of the Bible, and the literature is the body. Through the Book from the beautiful description of the Garden of Eden to the still more glorious vision of the Heavenly city, there runs a thread of gold which appears and reappears till in the New Testament, and especially in the gospels, the ground-work of narrative is covered with its splendid pattern and glittering embroidery. When the Lord said unto Abraham, "Get thee out of thy country and from thy kindred, and from thy father's house unto a land that I will show thee, and I will make of thee a great nation, and I will bless thee and make thy name great and thou shalt be a blessing"; or when the Lord passed before Moses and proclaimed, "The Lord, the Lord God, merciful and gracious, longsuffering and abundant in goodness and truth"; or when a saint from the fullness of his soul writes, "The Lord is my Shepherd I shall not want, He maketh me to lie down in green pastures, He leadeth me beside the still waters"; or when a prophet lifts up his testimony, "The mountains shall depart and the hills be removed, but My kindness shall not depart from thee, neither shall the covenant of My peace be removed, saith the Lord that hath mercy on thee"; or through the broken heart of Hosea, the Holy One of Israel cried in a passion of love, "How shall I give thee up Ephraim? How shall I deliver thee Israel . . . mine heart is turned within me, my repentings are kindled together. . . . I will heal their backslidings, I will love them freely for mine anger is turned away"—the note of the Evangel is as clearly sounded, though of course not so winningly, as when Jesus said, "Come unto Me all ye that labour and are heavy laden, and I will give you rest." It is not necessary to ask by whose lips came those words; they came from God, and they bear the impress of His heart. It is not necessary to fix their date; they are above all the ages eternal as the love of God. The classical Evangelical passages of the Bible are contemporaneous with all generations. The authority of the Evangel is beyond the reach of criticism as the soul is beyond the reach of physical analysis.

One may pause at this point and consider the question which has always been dear to the mystics, and makes a considerable appeal to our own age, whether truth must rest on the subjective experience of the believing Christian, or on the objective revelation of Holy Scripture. There is a pleasant story that David Hume, the sceptical philosopher, argued a whole evening with Dr. Jardine, of the Tron Kirk, Edinburgh, an earnest Evangelical, but Hume's good friend, to prove that no revelation was needed, and that the inner light is sufficient. When Hume left Jardine's house and went down the long stair which led to the street, he passed by mistake into the cellar, and Jardine hearing him wandering about in the darkness, came down and rescued him with a candle. " David, David," said Jardine, "what about the inner light now?" It is reported that Hume greatly enjoyed the situation, and was for once thankful that a light had been sent him from above. One must hold a balance between the authority of the historical revelation, which reveals God, and the authority of the moral sense which receives that revelation. A revelation were useless for any spiritual end, were it not assimilated by the man himself, so that he can say, " I know whom I have believed, and am persuaded," but this personal and experimental knowledge is always dependent, both for its beginning and its growth, upon the Bible revelation; without the gospels the Christian would never have known his Lord, and without the same gospels he could not grow in the knowledge of his Lord. When any one, therefore, on sceptical grounds considers the Bible unnecessary because he could find everything for himself without it, and when any one, on mystical grounds, speaks as if it were superseded because he has obtained all he needs from it, both are out of touch with reality. It is a matter of fact that the Bible has given a knowledge of God which has never been obtained elsewhere, and it is also a matter of fact that wherever mysticism has gone a-wandering away from the Bible it has landed in foolishness. For different reasons both the mystic and the sceptic making light of the Scriptures have landed in the cellar. The Bible is the sober standard of faith and conduct, and serves to correct the vagaries of heady self-will, and unlicensed fancies.

The authority of the Bible, when one goes to the root of the matter, whether we discriminate the spirit from the form, or estimate the force of that spirit, must stand in Christ. The Bible is a unity, and by that one means it is an articulated whole with many parts, and the spinal marrow and nervous system is the spirit of Christ. As the Bible, according to our idea of its development, culminates in Christ, so all its parts must be related to Christ. He is the

THE AUTHORITY OF THE BOOK 169

goal of its prophecy, and therefore the permanent element in prophecy is what has been fulfilled in Christ. Any imperfect conceptions of His person or limited ideas of His work which the prophets taught, fall to the ground, simply because He was greater than those ideas, and wider in His range. Whatever they prophesy truly of Him remains to illuminate and to expound both His person and His life. Whatever in the morality of the Jews before Christ was faulty or local, is abrogated, as it were automatically, by the teaching of Jesus; whatever is sound and lasting Jesus assimilates and spiritualizes. The Old Testament, therefore, has to be judged at every point by the standard of Christ, so that whatsoever is in harmony with the gospels is authoritative, and whatsoever is not, has no authority. By Christ are the Old Testament Scriptures judged, and either abrogated as temporary, or affirmed as eternal, and when they are affirmed they have the very authority of Christ's own words. The teaching of the apostles has also to be brought to the same standard. From time to time St. Paul turns aside from the high road of Christian thought to argue with Jews after a rabbinical fashion, or occasionally he conforms to Jewish rites. His teaching and his practice are not then binding on Christians, because they obviously differ from the teaching and practice of Jesus. As a rule he carries on the ideas of Jesus and carries forward Jesus' mission, and therefore his epistles grip the Christian reason and his example quickens the Christian conscience. The authority of the apostles is the authority of Christ. As a magnet will draw every morsel of steel from a heap of sand, so Jesus gathers to Himself from the wide and varied literature of the Bible the spiritual and eternal element of truth, and the preacher must therefore saturate his mind with the teaching of Jesus, that he may be able almost infallibly to distinguish between the body and soul of the Bible.

But Christ is not only the interpreter of the Bible, He is also the life of the Bible—and this must be firmly grasped by the minister. Withdraw Christ from the Bible as a living

THE AUTHORITY OF THE BOOK 171

personality and the Bible is only a superior religious literature. Place Christ in the centre of the Bible as its living heart, and the Bible is a spiritual force. Apart from Christ the Bible is like a picture painted on a sheet which can be studied with the aid of candles and whose beauty can be partially discerned. Place Christ behind it as an inner light, and the picture blazes into meaning and glory. He then is Moses who gives the law, and Joshua who conquers the land of Canaan, the King who judges the poor of the people, the Prophet who takes the veil from the face of God, the Priest who opens the way into the Holiest of all. He is the Shepherd of Israel who called His sheep by name; He is the mediator who brings the soul near unto God; He is the manna which cometh down from heaven, and the water from the stricken rock. Without Christ's person and life, without His death and resurrection, the promises of the Bible are like an elaborate covenant full of promises and benefits, but of no validity because unsealed. By Christ's cross and the red seal of His

Blood every invitation throughout the length and breadth of Holy Scripture is made efficacious, and every promise becomes " yea and amen." Just as the spiritual presence of Christ lends its only value to the Sacrament of the Lord's Supper, so the same presence invests with power the words of Holy Scripture. If any one receives the Sacrament in faith, he receives Christ; if any one hears Christ's word in faith, he also receives Christ. The Christian minister is not therefore merely an expositor of Scripture, he is the ambassador of Christ, and whatsoever is promised in Holy Scripture to the human soul, will be fulfilled in time and eternity, because it is promised by Christ Himself and He died and rose again to secure its certainty.

It follows that the authority of the Christian minister rests upon the same ground as the authority of the Bible, that it is spiritual and not formal, and that it is dependent not upon the signs of office, but upon the presence of Christ. There are indeed two conceptions of the ministry and it is well that we should decide which is true and upon which we are to work. One is that of the priest who belongs to a certain cast, and is set apart after a particular fashion, and obtains his grace from a specially appointed officer and whose chief act is the administration of the sacraments. The defects in this theory are first that the transmission of orders by Bishops in direct and unbroken line from the Apostles, cannot be proved historically. No scholar of importance will now pledge himself to the chain from the twelve to the Bishop of to-day, and if the pipe be cut anywhere the flow of grace has been broken. And secondly because it is impossible to prove this theory experimentally. No person can detect any difference in the man before and after he was ordained, nor any difference in the sacrament which he administers. You have simply to believe that he is connected without interruption with the Apostles, and that there resides in him a mysterious power which renders a sacrament valid; there is no evidence which can be called even plausible. According to the other theory the minister is a prophet who declares the message of God contained in the Holy Scriptures, and therefore received by the preacher from God Himself. Any one can trace the order of the prophets, for it depends not on the laying on of hands but upon the Evangel which they preach. They are not one by an invisible and unintelligible grace, but by the visible and effectual word in their mouths. Whether St. Paul and Pope Alexander VI belonged to the same order or not may be gravely questioned, but there is no question that the Apostle of the Gentiles and Charles Spurgeon had the same commission and were of the same kind. There is no difficulty in the prophet showing his commission and none in his hearers verifying it. Does he preach the Apostolic Gospel, Christ and Christ crucified, and do signs and wonders follow the preaching? Then every one may be certain that this man is preaching in the name and by the power of the Almighty. If one had seen St. Peter administer the sacraments in Jerusalem, he might have believed by his manner that he was fulfilling a sacred commission of Christ, but there would have been no objective proof.

THE AUTHORITY OF THE BOOK 175

If you had heard him preach the Gospel on the day of Pentecost, and seen three thousand people cast themselves on the mercy of the risen Lord, you would have known for certain that St. Peter was the chosen servant of Christ. He who opened the gates of the Kingdom to this multitude of penitent souls carried before all men the keys of the Lord. If any one believe that some ignorant and evil-living South American priest is a true minister of Christ, because he was ordained by a Bishop in a doubtful succession, then he is surely resting on a fancy which can never be confirmed, either by the intellectual or the moral sense; but if you believe that John Bunyan leading an innumerable multitude in the way everlasting by his "Pilgrim's Progress" is a veritable minister of the Lord Jesus, you are resting on facts which satisfy both the reason and the conscience. Can any person imagine for a single instant that if the Lord appeared in the midst of His Church on earth that He would welcome that priestly abject and reject the prophet of Bedford?

Whether the Word be higher than the Sacrament or the Sacrament than the Word, this is certain, that more people testify to the effect of single texts of Holy Scripture, than to the grace received in the sacrament. Multitudes which no man can number have set their seal in biographies, and in conversations to the great classical invitations of the Gospel. "Upon such a day," they say, "and by this word, light came to my soul." When John Knox, worn out by his strenuous life, lay a-dying, he ordered the fifteenth chapter of First Corinthians to be read over and over. "When this was ended," according to the account of his death, "he repeatedly said to himself, 'O what sweet and salutary consolation has the Lord afforded me by that chapter.' The following day about twelve o'clock he sat up in bed, but not long, for the weakness of his body did not suffer him; at three o'clock in the afternoon one of his eyes failed, nor did his tongue perform its office so expeditiously as formerly. At six o'clock however he said, 'Read the passages which I selected, especially the seventeenth chapter

of John, since there I have cast anchor.'"
One of the ablest prelates of the Anglican Church, and one of the chief reasoners in natural theology asked his chaplain to comfort him when he was near death, but was not satisfied by anything which was read, till the chaplain came to the passage, "It is a faithful saying, and worthy of all acceptation that Christ Jesus came into the world to save sinners, of whom I am chief." Upon that faithful saying, or rather upon the Lord behind that saying, Butler rested his soul. When Durham, one of the saints and theologians of the Scots Kirk came near the end of his journey, he was propped up in bed and an open Bible laid before him. "Find me," he said, "the eighth chapter of the Epistle to the Romans, and read me the last two verses. Place my hand on the words 'I am persuaded that neither death nor life nor angels nor principalities nor powers, nor things present, nor things to come, nor height nor depth nor any other creature shall be able to separate us from the love of God which is in Christ Jesus our Lord.'" A

little later an expression of deep peace and also of manifest joy settled on his face, and he passed within the veil.

Does not this experience of the saints, the men who really know about religion because they have been there, prove the inherent power of Holy Scripture to support the soul, and its divine authority? This is the Gospel of God, because it is the message which one would expect God to send, and which does for the soul what it needs. Between the soul in its necessity and the Bible in its Gospel there is a convincing correspondence, and therefore I should like in what remains of this lecture to make an earnest plea for more decided and unhesitating preaching. Is it not a misfortune that preaching has so largely lost the Positive Note? We stand aghast at the mental attitude of our fathers who allowed no open questions, comprehending everything from the origins to the ends of time, and casting good men out for heresy on subjects about which no human being could know anything. " God could or could not do this or that," they used to say and

THE AUTHORITY OF THE BOOK

beyond that point it is obvious none can travel. It was practical omniscience. We are much pleased with our own attitude—who do not seem at times to have any closed questions, being willing to discuss the existence of God or the resurrection of Christ or personal immortality in a neutral spirit with any person. There are no limits to our religious diffidence, and conciliatory concessions. We do well to congratulate ourselves upon our tolerance, provided that it arises from modesty about mysteries, or charity towards our fellow men, but we do far from well if we are tolerant because we do not think that there is any certainty possible in religion, or because we have no convictions to rouse our spirit. Preachers are affected by the atmosphere, and this to-day is anti-supernatural, so that without being conscious that their faith has weakened, they come to state truth in terms of worldly wisdom. The Personal God of the saints becomes the eternal Something or Other; He who was dead and is alive forevermore fades into "the Christ idea"; the miracles should really not be taken as fairy tales after the suggested discoveries of hypnotism; and immortality is saved from incredibility by the perpetually hopeful papers of the Psychical Society. One fears that in some quarters the pulpit has lost nerve. It may be that our fathers were too sure about everything; it would be an immense gain if their successors were absolutely sure about something.

If a preacher with the Bible in his hands is not positive, he has fallen short of his vocation. It is within his function to instruct and to defend, but he is chiefly a prophet with a message to the world from God. He is a witness to the supremacy of the soul, the reality of the unseen, the glory of the religious life—affirming with unfaltering voice those things which all men wish to believe and which they hold dimly in their minds. For the preacher of the Gospels the first qualification is not that he be learned or eloquent, but that he believe; and whatever be the case with other men he must believe with the marrow of his bones. If this be impossible then let him become anything he

THE AUTHORITY OF THE BOOK 181

pleases, but not a preacher; and if doubts settle upon him, let him face and master them in secret—in the wilderness with God, and stand before his fellow men with unclouded face. There are enough men to ventilate doubts without the preacher's assistance. From him the world expects faith, and the dynamic of one man believing with all his mind and all his heart, is incalculable; it is a reservoir of life in the midst of a bloodless and worn-out society. Doubt can be got anywhere; faith ought to be supplied by the pulpit.

Of course the preacher ought to be positive about the right things, and to distinguish between the facts and the theories of Christianity. Our faith has its being amid certain realities in the sphere of religion: such as revelation, that God has spoken to us in the gospel; the Deity of Christ—that Christ is the Son of the Father in a sense which can be asserted of no other man; Redemption—that Christ by His sacrifice delivers the soul from the power of sin; the Holy Ghost—that God ministers grace to the soul by His indwelling Spirit; the life to come—that there will be a future existence with moral distinctions. Around those facts gather a number of theories, such as Inspiration and Substitution. The facts are religion, the theories are theology, and while the facts should be declared with assurance, the theories should be advanced with diffidence. It is one thing to insist on the message of God springing out of Holy Scripture as its very flower and fruit, and another to explain how it was given; one thing to preach Christ as a Saviour and another to settle whether He offered an exact equivalent for the penalty of our sin. When one is positive on the radiant facts of our Christian faith, he is on strong ground; when he is dogmatic on the results of theological science, he is at a disadvantage. If one insists on the virtue of Christ's sacrifice to redeem the soul from the grip of sin, he is resting upon experience; when he suggests the principle of the Atonement, he has entered into the region of speculation. He is now showing the picture with the help of a candle in order to illuminate its shadows.

One candle after serving its turn has burned out and has been replaced by another, and no doubt each candle had its own value. Every theory of the Atonement, from that of the Fathers according to which Christ paid a price to the devil for the ransom of His people, to the modern Evangelical one called the substitutionary, is a contribution to the better understanding of the facts. With this distinction in our minds theology becomes the handmaid of truth, but it is on truth as declared in the Bible and not on theology as created in the study, the minister of Christ must be positive.

We ought to be positive in the right spirit. When a preacher offers the beautiful verities of the Bible as the heritage of our race, then the soul is captivated and made eager for their acceptance; when a preacher gathers together the elements of the Christian faith and demands that his hearers should accept them with an alternative of punishment, then the Evangel is held as a pistol to the head, and imperfectly sanctified human nature is apt to rebel. Preaching which attacks a man's belief irritates; preaching which transfigures a man's beliefs, conciliates. Is your hearer an agnostic?—assume that he longs to know the nameless God, and drop the veil from the face of Christ. Has he a besetting sin?—exhibit to him the opposite virtue in Christ, whose Purity like a fire burns up our dross. Is he a slave of this present world?—let the glory of the eternal cast into the shade the glitter of the temporal. Let the preacher be ever full of charity, believing that every man is willing to exchange his error, which is a half truth, for the whole truth, and that every man in his best moments passionately desires to be free from his sin. Preaching should never be destruction; it ought ever to be fulfillment, the shining of light into a dark room, the rushing of a tide up the empty channel of a river, against which there is no resistance, with which comes exceeding joy.

Above all speakers the Christian minister has good grounds for being positive, and ought to have them in his mind when he faces his fellow men from the pulpit. He gives a pledge of authority as he stands behind the open Bible, for beyond all question the Bible has a voice of peculiar majesty. Like the deep mellow sound of a bell floating out from a cathedral tower on the violet sky of Italy, and arresting for a brief moment at least the confused babel of the Carnival below, the utterances of this Book fall on the restless questions, and fretful anxieties of the soul. Hearers are of a sudden hushed into reverence, and are inclined to submission, not by the ipse dixit of a fallible preacher, but because the mouth of the Lord hath spoken it. What the preacher says will certainly be verified in the experience of his hearers, since the inner story of humanity is ever the same. If he describes any particular sin which is devastating his own life, many of his people will tremble because he has gone through the secret ways of their heart, and with the candle of the Lord. If he commends the divine grace which in his sore strait has comforted him, he may give his imagination full scope, for this man and that will desire to rise in his place and declare that the same Lord has done yet greater things for him. We speak from life to life, from conscience to conscience, from heart to heart with unerring correspondence.

And the preacher of the Evangel does not stand alone before his audience, for his single puny figure is flung into relief against the background of the saints of all ages—the Catholic Church of God. They also have grasped the promises and trusted in God; they also have made their venture, and have not been put to confusion. Christ afar off or near has been to them all their desire and their salvation. When the preacher makes his appeal for Christ, he wakens an echo from distant places and many centuries. Abraham, going forth into a strange country on the strength of the promise, cries Amen; Isaiah, writing his fifty-third chapter, joins in the word; St. John lifts his head from Jesus' bosom to add his testimony; St. Paul raises his chained arm to bear witness to the Lord. Unto the vision of faith the heavens are opened, and there is seen a multitude no man can number who have washed their robes and made them white in the blood of the Lamb, and unto the ear of faith the preacher's voice is drowned in music like unto the sound of many waters—"Blessing and honour and glory and power be unto Him that sitteth upon the throne, and unto the Lamb forever and ever."

LECTURE V
THE STYLE OF THE BOOK

LECTURE V

THE STYLE OF THE BOOK

AS the range of the Bible is wide as humanity so its style is wide as literature. There is indeed no form of speech of which its writers have not availed themselves. You have philosophy in Job, history in the Pentateuch, poetry in the Psalms, and biography in the Gospels. You have the sententiousness of the books of wisdom, and the glancing freedom of the Epistles. Every form of humour except the jocularity of the West is found in the Bible, from the irony of the prophets to the gentle humour of Jesus in the parable of the midnight visitor and the unjust judge; the illustration of the children's games, and the repartee of the physician who visits the sick and not the whole. With this comprehensive example before him in his text-book, the preacher in his sermon is entitled to use every form of human speech, provided he be never trifling or vulgar or irreverent or inhuman. If he employs humour it must be with delicacy and reserve. He is not to be condemned if he provokes a smile—people often smile because what is said is so perfectly true, not because it is amusing. He is to be condemned if he raises a laugh, for people only laugh when they are amused. While the Evangel may have every other kind of human quality, it should never be made amusing. If there is one man more to be despised than another it is the jester in the pulpit; he may gather a crowd of groundlings for a season, but he has insulted his high commission. I do not say that the minister is to be envied who has no sense of humour, for his touch will be heavy and, which surely is an irony of things, he may become grotesque, and when he intends to be most solemn may be most absurd. But I do say that the man who has this tricky gift, and is called to the Christian ministry, must bit and bridle it when he is engaged in his sacred duty. If he can use it to ridicule folly and to expose sin, to check the absurdities of good people, and to win men's hearts, then it is a valuable instrument in his hands, as it was in the hands of his Master. But if humour has only the effect of lowering the dignity of the ambassador of Christ when in the discharge of his high duties, or belittling the authority of his message, then humour becomes a hindrance and an offense. When a congregation watches for the jocose passages with which its coarser palate is fed and pays no attention to the seriousness between, then surely the vainest and shallowest of preachers must see that he is playing the fool, and doing so in the face of heaven.

Just as critics insist that poetry of the first order—the work of Dante or of Milton, is distinguished by what is called the grand note, so preaching ought to differ from a literary lecture or a platform speech by a certain indescribable but recognizable majesty of tone, and this can be best caught from the Bible itself. Bunyan illustrates this style of speech in its highest degree, combining as no other man outside the Bible has done grandeur with simplicity. But simple men, without education or genius have caught the infection of this dignity, and when they spake of spiritual things were raised above themselves and had the tongue of the Prophets and Apostles. The Bible has through its length and breadth the sound of eternity, and by that one means that it is never provincial in its spirit, but universal, and the great preaching which is saturated with the Bible spirit is always imperial. Herein there is a great difference between two kinds of preachers—the one who preaches to the times and the other who, like Archbishop Leighton, asks permission "to preach Jesus Christ and eternity." The mind of the imperial preacher breathes its native air on that lofty table-land where the saints live with God, and occupies itself with those eternal verities which effect the human soul in every age. It is his habit to dwell upon the character of God, the impurity of sin, the stainless righteousness of spiritual law, upon the everlasting love and unfathomable wisdom of our heavenly Father, upon the coming of the Lord Jesus into human life and the epic of salvation from His Incarnation to His Resurrection, upon the indwelling and patient work of the Holy Ghost, upon the unqualified freedom of the divine mercy, and the unsearchable riches of the divine grace, upon the anxieties of the soul in her quest for God, and the sacred experiences of the religious life, upon the awfulness of judgment and the glory of the life everlasting. Amid those high themes, this preacher makes his spiritual home as the eagle builds her nest in the clefts of unscaled cliffs; from such heights he studies the plains of human life, and descends to preach to his fellows. His words may be simple and easily understood by the people, yet they will have caught the tone of the unseen world. The preacher himself will have the unconscious dignity of one who is keeping high company and he will speak with the indescribable authority of one with whom God holds converse. Such preaching is not confined to any environment or period, it belongs to no nation or time, it is ageless preaching.

Another type of preacher, though from time to time he may climb the heights, and although he may be ever conscious of their wide view, builds by preference his intellectual home amid the circumstances of human life and the interests of his own age. What he studies with sympathetic mind is that life of man which is "such a comedy to those who think, such a tragedy to those who feel." What fills his imagination is not so much the "New Jerusalem coming down from God out of heaven, prepared as a bride adorned for her husband"; it is rather his own city made clean and glad. What rouses him to a white heat is not the insolent rebellion of man against God, but some deed of political unrighteousness. The ideal he holds out before men is not so much the vision of God, dear to the heart of the mystic, as a perfect manhood according to the stature of Christ. The method of religion upon which he fondly dwells is not,

"The silent life of prayer,
Praise, fast, and alms,"

but the service of man in philanthropic enterprise or municipal politics. For his inspiration outside the Bible he would rather turn to the last book on social service than to à Kempis, whom he is apt to consider a type of religious selfishness, or to Pascal who repels him by his intellectual austerity. His ear is so besieged by the voices of men calling for help that it cannot always catch the voice of God, and he is so immersed in the practice of religion that he has no leisure for its research. When he speaks to his fellows this prophet does not come from a lonely retreat, but rises in the market-place, his accent is that of to-day, and he speaks of that which has been buzzing up and down the streets. Every one is glad to hear him, and understands what he intends, for his sermons are a glorified echo of what men are discussing in the club, and in their homes, what is being written in contemporary books, and monthly magazines. His sermons may have quotations from the masters of thought and may refer at times to the great movements which have made history, but they are certain to be rich in local colour, and to show the soil through which they have been running. As one turns over the leaves he catches the name of a living politician, of a popular pressman, of an infamous criminal, of a fashionable novelist; he finds allusions to a scandal in high life, to a controversy between two Churches, to the last attack on Christianity by some dashing free lance, and to the compensation of publicans. The sermons are charged with the life of to-day, and the hearer is perfectly at home : he understands to the last word what is said to him, and is never taken into solitary places where he would be ill at ease; he knows exactly what he ought to do and it is never any hopeless ideal. This is contemporary rather than eternal preaching, provincial rather than imperial, less rather than more Biblical. It has the atmosphere of the Bible.

When one makes this distinction he ought to admit that the gain is not all on one side. If the imperialist has a wider outlook and a firmer grasp of principles, he may fail to touch the multitude who are weary with the greatness of his ideas, and may not be a force in present day questions, because he does not relate them to his heavenly doctrine. It is possible to be a master in pure mathematics and yet to be helpless in physics, and indeed to reach that state of mind which considers any application of mathematics to be their degradation. There are minds whose enthusiasm is confined to the study and evaporates in the practice of life, to whom ideas are everything and men are nothing. They produce sermons which for abstract speculation suggest the fourth dimension, but for any human relation might as well be preached in Mars as in this present world. It is no reproach to the ordinary man accustomed to the domestic life of the valley, that he is not at home on the top of a lonely crag with this intrepid climber; it does not mean that he is unspiritual, it may not even mean that he is unintellectual, it simply means that he is human. And it also means that in this case the preacher in paying his tribute to the divinity of the Bible has lost touch with its humanity, and that the Christ he preaches is a ghost and not the Son of Mary.

On the other hand there is no question that the provincial preacher has an undeniable opportunity and has wrought great works. There is no power like speech in the conflict of affairs, and preachers have often turned the battle in the gate by sermons in which every sentence told upon a present situation; they have beaten down unrighteousness, overthrown tyranny, delivered the oppressed and established the kingdom of God in their city and in their land. The sermons a year afterwards were antiquated and obsolete, and therefore, one sees, belong to a different order from that of Jesus and the Apostles. But who can say that they had not served their purpose, and generations to come who never heard of them would reap their fruits. When Knox preached in St. Giles he dealt with the dangers of the day, and the duty laid upon his countrymen, and if there be few who would care to read his St. Giles sermons, yet as he says himself, "the Doctrin was proper for the tyme," and "in applicatioun qahairof he was so special and vehement," that even Maitland of Lethington said in mockage, "We mon now forget ourselffis and beir the barrow to buyld the housses of God." Perhaps it does not matter much that the sermon itself should be forgotten if it shakes the life of a nation. Calvin was the perfect type of a thinker, and with his dead hand he still grips the reason of the Reformed Churches, but his administration left no trace. Knox was no scholar, and his sermons could not be read to-day, but in his time they were as the sound of many trumpets, and in Knox a nation realized itself, and came into its kingdom. Wisdom is justified of her children. It remains, however, if God has given him genius, the imperial preacher, in the Bible sense, with the range of Isaiah or St. Paul, addresses not only his own generation, but has generations unborn at his command. So long as there are sinners, and the English language is spoken, Bunyan's great sermon on "Jerusalem Sinners Saved," will be read with wet eyes and tender hearts. You do not need to know a circumstance of the period to feel the force of that sermon, you only require to know your own heart and the infinite pathos of human life. Mr. Spurgeon addressed all kinds and conditions of men and the sermons preached fifty years ago are a living message to-day, and will not be out of date when the twentieth century is drawing to its close. John Henry Newman and Robertson of Brighton have made a permanent contribution to our religious literature, and from the past, South and Jeremy Taylor, two very different men, still speak to us. Those preachers have passed but they have not perished; they have won their place among the immortals, because they have dealt worthily with immortality. It is the disability of the provincial preacher that though he may work marvels by the grace of God in his day, and is carried aloft like a successful general upon the shields of his enthusiastic soldiers, yet he does not remain. The life goes out from his war cry because the battle has been fought, and the meaning out of his illustrations because the circumstances have changed. Between the two kinds of sermons, there will be the same difference as between Cicero's "De Senectute" and his "Letters to Atticus." The one can be understood everywhere and in every time, the other is the kind of book which in a generation requires to be edited, and at our rate of living would fade in six months. Chrysostom and Massillon, to take instances far apart, were soaked in the life of their day and dealt frankly with its sins, but the homilies of the one and the sermons of the other are as convincing as when the golden-mouthed orator moved audiences to tumults of applause at Antioch, and the Court preacher so adroitly rebuked Louis XIV that the king left the Chapel dissatisfied not with the preacher but with himself.

As we are living in a day when men are more concerned about the things that are temporal than those which are eternal, it is a snare for the preacher to speak to his people in the dialect of the moment, rather than in the language of the ages, and to attract audiences by treating the incidental affairs of public life which is ever changing like a kaleidoscope, and to be afraid to touch the profound experiences of the soul which is the air of eternity. Certainly the preacher should be in touch with his day, and Amos spoke to his generation, if any prophet ever did, but it is well for the preacher enveloped by our secular spirit to remember that burning subjects soon die into white ashes, and that when this artificial fire has perished audiences also grow cold and seek some other hearth, while congregations which are fed with the living bread, grow more receptive every day, and will not lightly forsake the teacher who has satisfied the hunger of the soul. The ideal preacher is he who in his sermon can so relate time to eternity that he shall be able to deal with the most commonplace affairs from the height of the loftiest principles. It is characteristic of the Bible teachers that they connected every duty with the eternal law of righteousness, and lifted the commonplaces of life to the level of worship. Amos was indignant with

Israel not only because they had sinned so wantonly in the excess of luxury and in the oppression of the poor, but because they had done all this after receiving such grace at the hands of God, and he warned his people that according to the richness of their privilege, would be the heaviness of their punishment. "You only have I known of all the families of the earth, therefore I will punish you for all your iniquities." Because the children of Israel were a family which God had brought up from the land of Egypt, therefore they ought to be humble, self-denying, sympathetic, obedient. After the same fashion St. Paul in his exhortations to the early Christians condescends upon the humblest details of daily duty, but he makes them the outcome of the life that is hid with Christ in God. After his magnificent exposition of the doctrine of the Resurrection, and after sounding the trumpet of victory over death and sin he goes on, "Therefore, my beloved brethren, be ye steadfast, unmovable, always abounding in the work of the Lord, forasmuch as ye know that your labour is not in vain in the

Lord." And immediately thereafter, "Now concerning the collection for the saints." There is no truth so profound, but it can be brought to bear on the most modest affairs of life, just as iron bridges are built by a formula of pure mathematics, and no task so practical but it can be informed by the highest knowledge, just as scientific breeders of wheat call to their assistance the calculations of the mathematician. All knowledge is one and no man to-day can be an expert physiologist unless he have a working knowledge of mathematics and certain discoveries by a botanist have been used by the investigators into the origin of cancer. All life is one; the life of Christ before the throne throbs in the soul of the humblest believer, and the great sacrifice which Christ accomplished is repeated as often as one of us serves another in the lowliest ministry of earth. As George Herbert, the perfect pastor of the English Church, pleasantly says:

> "A servant with this clause,
> Makes drudgery divine.
> Who sweeps a room, as for Thy laws,
> Makes that and the action fine."

THE STYLE OF THE BOOK

There are preachers who are extra-spiritual, because they do not follow principles into practice, and there are preachers who are extra-secular, because they insist on practice without principles. But there is another order, and in our day Dr. Dale of Birmingham was perhaps its most conspicuous representative, who are able to wed principle and practice together, as St. Paul did when in the Roman Epistle he passes easily from the heights of God's purposes to the duty of Christian hospitality. And that preacher has come near perfection, who can make the springs hidden amid the everlasting hills pour their water into the valley beneath, to make green its meadows and to drive the peasant's humble wheel.

While the most striking feature of the Bible style is its combination of the eternal and the temporal, there are certain qualities which it may help us to note in detail and which may pass with advantage into the texture of the sermon. One is intelligibility, or interest. Whether it be a prophet addressing his generation on the sins of the day, or an apostle declaring the gospel in a Gentile market-place, or the Master giving His most profound discourses, one knows what the speaker means. The Bible style may on occasion be oratorical, or it may be familiar; it may be kind or it may be severe; it may touch on the mysteries of life or on life's simplest offices. It is always unaffected and straightforward, it always employs the current speech of the day which the man upon the street can understand, and not preciosities of literature which only the student in his study can taste. It has dignity without pomposity, sublimity without subtlety, spirituality without mistiness. As George Herbert writes of the Bible,

> "'Tis heaven in perspective; and the bliss
>   Of glory here,
>   If anywhere,
> By saints on earth anticipated is,
>   Whilst faith to every word
>   A being doth afford."

Bible language is impressive by an inherent grandeur and perfect in its felicitous taste, but it is always plain, so that he who runneth can read, and the wayfaring man though he be a fool cannot err therein. It is indeed a paradox that the style of the Bible is much simpler than that of the commentaries written to expound it, and one keenly appreciates the experience of the good old woman who was presented with a commentary on the gospels and asked whether it had helped her to understand. "Well," she said, "the large print above (which was the gospel text) I can easily follow, but the small print below (which was the illumination of the commentator) fairly drives me stupid." The common people heard Christ gladly for various reasons, but largely because they understood Him. And they understood Him because He did not use the terms of the rabbis, but the words of every-day life, and because He did not take abstruse illustrations but employed the panorama upon which their eyes were looking.

Our Master beyond any prophet or apostle must always be the chief model for the preacher, and the fascination of Jesus' speech can be traced to various sources, but never is He more engaging than in His prodigal use of the parable. Certain minds are so governed by its abstractions that they can never connect an idea with the system of things, but keep it in a place apart; others are so destitute of imagination that they never catch any analogy between the spiritual world and the natural. Such minds in the pulpit labour under a perpetual disability, for they depend for the exposition of truth either on the processes of reason or the deductions of tradition; their teaching may be valuable, it will always be ineffectual. As Jesus looked out on nature and on life, the scene was shot through as in a transparency by the unseen. No truth of religion ever came to Him naked and austere, but in a comely shape and clothed with fair colours; no practice of religion but realized itself before His eyes in the habits of daily living. This outward show with its rising and setting sun, its pasture lilies and its growing corn, its viewless wind and flocks of careless birds, was a sacrament—the sign of the sacred mysteries of the soul. This varied human life with its

THE STYLE OF THE BOOK

fishermen in their boats, its farmers sowing the seed, its working women busy with household labour, its rich men giving feasts, was the rehearsal of the history of the kingdom of God. The Gospel of Jesus can be found in the parables, which remain the most beneficent assistant which style has afforded to thought.

The parable always interests and although some learned and pious persons seem to consider it a duty to weary an audience, the first aim of our Lord was to win and to conciliate. It was His custom to pass from reason to illustration, as one turns from the dusty road into the fields. He came quite as quickly to His destination, and distance was forgotten on account of the beauty of the way. Neither poetry nor pathos, neither eloquence nor argument, will so surely catch the ear or hold the attention as a tale. One may hazard the guess that as soon as the two first human beings realized themselves and one another, Adam told Eve a story. When the last two huddle themselves together on the frozen earth they will tell the things which have been. It is with a story that childhood is soothed, with a story that the cares of age are relieved. As Jesus preaches, a panorama of life unfolds itself, ever illuminated by the inner life. We watch the farmer going down his fields and throwing his seed from side to side, and the tiny pickles falling on the four kinds of soil which divide between them human character. We detect the treacherous neighbour stealing through the field in the night-time and sowing the evil seed of tares among the wheat; we stand on the lake shore as the fishermen draw in their net with toil and strain and separate the fluttering spoil into the good and the bad. We admire the glitter of the goodly pearl in the merchant's hand, and are concerned until he has secured it at a great price; we are excited as the plow strikes on the buried treasure-chest and the fortunate peasant tears open the lid; we follow with sympathetic interest the shepherd as he seeks for his lost sheep, and the woman as she hunts for her lost coin. We are indignant at the Pharisee's self-righteous prayer in the

Temple, and are vastly pleased when justice is done to the unmerciful servant; we also wait in the market-place with the unemployed labourers and approve the reward given to the men who have made good use of their talents. True to the principle of action which controls the whole revelation of Holy Scripture, Jesus calls His hearers to consider the busy life of men, and in the midst of vivid and varied scenes we are taught with delight and ease the deepest truths.

Another quality of the Bible style which should be imitated in the pulpit is its reasonableness. Throughout its length and breadth the Bible deals respectfully with men in the sense that it endeavours to win their consent as intellectual and moral beings. They may be brow-beaten by dogma, but they are not bullied by the Bible; they are not commanded to believe whether they understand or not, far less because the truth is incredible; they are asked to accept the truth because it is high and noble and in keeping with supreme reason. The controversy in the days of the prophets was between a reasonable God and an unreasonable people. "Hear O heavens and give ear O earth for the Lord hath spoken, I have nourished and brought up children, and they have rebelled against Me. The ox knoweth his owner, and the ass his master's crib, but Israel doth not know, My people doth not consider." What God asks in the Bible is that people should think and if they will only take the trouble of thought, they will both believe aright and do aright. The typical fool in the Bible is not an uneducated person, he is a sinner; sin in the Bible is many things but chiefly it is a tremendous mistake—it is missing the mark. The sinner has failed and made a ruin of life. Jesus did not complain that men were doubtful and amazed about His new doctrine; that they asked questions and did not at once make up their mind. He was ready to explain anything, and desired every one to be fully persuaded, and if He dealt sharply with intellectual hypocrites, He was the most patient of teachers to a sincere sceptic. We do less than justice to the contents of our religion when we represent them as commonplace like the multiplication table without mysteries and without surprises; we also do less than justice to the reason of our fellow men when we demand that they should receive every truth of Christianity at the point of the bayonet. Christianity is the most profound revelation within our horizon, and he who would possess its fullness, must not be afraid to ask questions, and the preacher must not weary answering them till his hearers' reason be fully persuaded. When one is commending Christian truth from the pulpit and when one is verifying it in the pew, both preacher and hearer should be careful to use the most convincing test and should take note of the Master's own method of conviction. When He was on His defense, with what evidences did He support His gospel, and with what plea did He win its acceptance? When His opponents denied what He said, upon what aids did He fall back? Never upon the accumulated theology of the schools, which was such an armoury of weapons for the Rabbis, and which Jesus absolutely ignored, and very rarely upon mere logic, that kind of argument which checkmates you according to rules in a game of words, although Jesus occasionally condescended to worst the Pharisees by this method. Sometimes He did appeal to texts, but only when He was speaking to men with whom the appeal to texts was an end of all controversy. Occasionally He availed Himself of His divine right of assertion and with a " verily, verily " laid down the law of truth, but He never did so in order to silence the human reason but to rouse it to its highest power. His chief weapon when He appeals to the human soul was the absolute reasonableness of His Gospel when tried by the experience of human life. " You cannot accept My representation of God," He says in effect when making His great defense in the fifteenth chapter of St. Luke's Gospel, " or the divinity of My mission. You cannot believe that God will deal with sinners as I have taught, or that I ought to treat them as I do. Very good, then I will ask this single question. Compare the action of God with the best action of your own life, and tell Me if God as

THE STYLE OF THE BOOK

I teach Him is not doing exactly as you would wish to do when you are at your best, and whether My method of salvation is not in keeping with the principles of life? Look round and behold My gospel in action; look within yourselves and see if I be not vindicated. What man of you?"—the decision is left in our own hands. Jesus has appealed to our moral reason; by that reason He is ever willing to be justified.

When Jesus appeals to the shepherd before Him who has lost his sheep and the woman who has lost her coin and the father who has lost his son, He brings His teaching out of the air and places it upon the earth, and this is a very great gain for simple folk. Are we not all apt to regard the doctrines of Christianity as propositions, laid down by divine inspiration through the writers of Holy Scripture or by the councils of the Church, which we ought to accept whether we believe them to be true or not? We imagine them a revelation of things which we never could have discovered and which when discovered we have no right to judge, because they are not within the range of our knowledge and are not a part of our experience. Are we accustomed, as Jesus suggests, to believe that life human and divine are one, that what is right with God is right with man, and what is true with man is true with God, and that therefore religious truth will be confirmed before our eyes by the laws of human life? Jesus' revelation is not so much the unveiling of a spiritual fact which is beyond our consciousness, as it is the unveiling of our mind to the fact which, when once seen, we can see always. He did not ask men to believe anything which they could not verify in their own soul, but He did insist that if His Gospel was sanctioned by the action and thought of human life on its highest plain, that it was true. According to our Master no doctrine therefore makes any just claim upon our mind which is not an induction from human experience, and any doctrine which is condemned by human experience is to be rejected.

Observe in passing how the application of this Bible principle—whether it confirm or remove doctrine, will tend to the establishment of the Christian faith. Among the doctrines which have been held by all Christians with a few exceptions is the Incarnation of the Son of God. Doubtless there is no one who would not wish to believe that God Himself came into this welter of sin and sorrow for our aid, but it comes over the mind that for the Almighty to condescend so far, and to limit Himself to human nature, is a thing not only mysterious but incredible. Then we turn to human experience, and ask what one of us at his highest would wish to do in similar circumstances. Suppose that at the upper end of a city a man is living in a house defended against disease and want, reinforced by every comfort, and gladdened by every beauty, and that at the other end of the city men and women are living in hovels, without sunshine, without air, beset by temptations, worn out by labour, weakened by disease, without joy, without knowledge, without hope, would you not expect that man if he were of the nobler order to make the case of his suffering brethren his own, and if he went so far as to go down and live with his poor kinsmen, sharing the same lot, placing himself under the same conditions, save that he carried from the past an immunity from evil, would that not be from the point of view of the moral reason, a noble and becoming action, would it not be one worthy of God Himself? Was not this what God did through the Incarnation? And is it to be supposed that He alone may not make sacrifices or that He alone should be safeguarded from sorrow? Must not the cross be also in the heart of God? When Jesus teaches the love of God and declares that in His chief sacrifice He is fulfilling the will of God, He carries our judgment with Him.

"The very God! think, Abib; dost thou think?
So, the All-Great, were the All-Loving, too —
So, through the thunder comes a human voice
Saying, 'O heart I made, a heart beats here!
Face My hands fashioned, see it in Myself!
Thou hast no power nor mayst conceive of Mine,
But love I gave thee, with Myself to love,
And thou must love Me who have died for thee!'
The madman saith he said so: it is strange."

Let us apply this principle to a doctrine

which has ever been a stumbling-block, and which has been the opprobrium of Calvinism, that of reprobation. It may, let us grant, be proved by a few statements torn bleeding out of their contexts and saturated with local feeling, that God intended certain men to be condemned to everlasting destruction and that nothing they could do would be of any service to deliver them from their doom. But one cannot bear the thought that our heavenly Father should so deal with any of His children, and certainly if He did so one could never trust Him again. We turn to life and find that a father may have to distinguish between his children, treating prodigals sharply for their own good, and for the sake of his family; that he may have to deny the management of affairs to ignorant children and to place them under the charge of those who are wiser. We also find, however, that all such distinctions are intended for the good even of those who suffer, and that an earthly father of the best kind is ever doing the wisest and kindest he knows for his children. We look out on history and see that the Jewish nation received special favour in order that they might be the means of special blessing, and that the gifts bestowed upon certain people, the ability of the statesman, the courage of the soldier, the riches of the capitalist, are intended for the welfare of the nation. And with this life both of the family and of the nation before us, full of comprehensive fatherly government, we see the doctrine of sovereignty vindicated but the doctrine of reprobation condemned, and we throw it aside as a slander upon God.

Our Master was ever in touch with life, and therein He differs from the scribes of every age. His paradoxes may startle you; His commandments try you, His deep sayings solemnize you, His searching words offend you; but your higher self, your intellectual and moral sense, is never outraged or driven into revolt by Christ. You can never say of His teaching, it is an offense to my conscience, it is a contradiction of my experience. He ever fulfills the highest function of the pulpit to express our noblest thoughts and to explain our deepest feelings. Take twenty representative men of all ages and all schools, ask them to leave their peculiar views outside the room as one leaves his outer garment in the hall, and then when they are all cleansed from partial counsel, place before them one of Christ's sermons—it does not matter which, they all fulfill the same condition. Ask this commission of various interests, whether they object to anything; it is impossible. You dare not ask them if the discourse is able; it were a profanity. You would not ask them if it were orthodox; it were an irrelevancy. It is true; that is the conclusion from beginning to end, beautifully and perfectly true. Christendom has been torn in pieces by the doctrines of Christians, yet there has not risen a man of note inside or outside of Christianity, who has denied anything Christ said, or found it in his heart to criticise Christ. He could not because our human experience responds to the touch of Christ like the strings of a harp to the harper. This reasonableness has been the felicitous monopoly of Christ, and the more reasonable His ministers are the nearer they come to their Master.

The third quality of the Bible style is sympathy; each department of speech, judicial, political, commercial and scientific, has its own characteristic note. So has the preaching of the Gospel from the days of St. Paul to those of Whitfield, through a long line of preachers with the most varied gifts speaking to the most varied times. Certainly there is no kind of style which cannot be illustrated from Bible literature, from the speculation of Job to the cynicism of Ecclesiastes, from the declamation of the prophets to the mysticism of the Apocalypse. The preacher is justified in using argument, imagination, sarcasm, pathos, for has he not to win complete humanity to Christ? But through it all he ought to be tender, gracious, conciliatory, charitable. His speaking should be set to the key, "Comfort ye, comfort ye My people, saith your God, speak ye comfortably to Jerusalem"; "Come now and let us reason together, saith the Lord, though your sins be as scarlet they shall be as white as snow, though they be red like crimson, they shall be as wool"; "O Jerusalem, Jerusalem, thou that killest the prophets and stonest them which are sent unto thee, how often would I have gathered thy children together even as a hen gathereth her chickens under her wing, and ye would not." Men are like foolish sheep, miserable and lost, who must be found; they are wayward children who must be brought home. The Bible is the defender of the oppressed and a friend of the prisoner; it pities the sick, and has endless promises for the sorrowful; its favoured children are the widow, the orphan, the poor and the broken-hearted. Jesus Himself lived in a narrow home, and led a struggling life; He took His illustrations for the most part from narrow circumstances and ever turned aside to cases of trouble; He was the man of sorrows and acquainted with grief. One of the great ends of the pulpit is to console men and to put heart into them, to assure them of the victory of righteousness, of the fellow feeling of Jesus with us, of the blessedness of the departed and the glory of our Father's house.

The light from the open gate of the city should be ever streaming across the sermon. The most unbiblical preacher is a hard man, the most biblical is one whose heart is full of tears. If the preacher has to denounce iniquity, let him not do so savagely; if he has to preach punishment let him do so pitifully; let him rather turn men from badness to goodness by the allurements of heaven, than by the horrors of hell. It is not in keeping with the love of God, or with the nobility of human nature, that men should be dragooned into faith. The messenger speaking in the name of the Eternal Father to his sons, however wayward or however ignorant, should assume that the real self in every man is his better self, and that in every one there is a core of goodness—the defaced image of God,—and that every man recognizes the good and would fain himself be like it.

While the preacher should appeal to reason, because Christianity is supremely reasonable, yet it is not wise for him to give himself to the methods of philosophy, or to spend his strength in vindicating the primary conceptions of religion. He had better remember that religion deals with things that are assumed and have not to be proved, with intuitions rather than propositions. The preacher should appeal to conscience, for Christianity fulfills itself in godly living, but he had better remember that there is nothing a man knows more clearly than his duty, and nothing which he finds more difficult to do. He must not therefore discourage or weary his people by arid and doctrinaire ethical sermons. It is not more knowledge but more power that humanity needs, and therefore the office of preaching is to do more than enlighten the reason or quicken the conscience; its supreme effort is to capture the affections and to make them the motive power of goodness. Religion rules over the whole of a man's nature, but its throne is set in the heart; when a man loves the best with his whole heart, he will not wish to do the worst. That which holds his heart will govern his life, and therefore the preacher of Christ will speak much of love; he will be ever reminding men, under many images and by many unexpected approaches, of the sorrow of the Father who has lost His children, and greatly misses them; of the love of God who has pitied this sinful world and has not spared His own Son for its salvation; of the sufferings of the Lord Jesus in the via dolorosa of His life from Bethlehem to Calvary, and of the patience of the Holy Ghost as He strives in human hearts. His endeavour is not to batter down the walls of human nature by blatant threatenings or to capture the citadel by some brilliant assault of cleverness, for this were to win a dangerous victory and to put the garrison to shame. His chosen aim will be to bring it to pass that the defenders of the fortress will be so taken by the offers of the besieging and friendly force that they will themselves open the great gates with hearty good will, and bid the King of Glory enter in. And the preacher has finished his task, and is satisfied when he sees his Lord seated on the throne of a willing and obedient soul for this is the final and unchangeable victory of salvation.

LECTURE VI
THE USE OF THE BOOK

LECTURE VI

THE USE OF THE BOOK

EVERY age has its own fashions and the pulpit is not independent of the spirit of the day. There was a time within the memory of middle-aged men when not only was the text taken as a matter of course from the Bible, but the sermon was drawn from the same source and might indeed be nothing but a cento of passages from the Scriptures. In our time if a text is quoted from the Bible it is often only a motto—a tuning of the subject like the ballads with which Scott and Kipling start their chapters. With this sonorous and becoming convention the modern puts off from the shore of Bible truth and sails upon his adventurous voyage wherever the prevailing wind may carry him. Our fathers might not know the exact theme on which their minister would address them, but they were certain that it would be within the province of religion. We are informed in the advertisement column of Saturday's newspaper on what our minister will speak, and are quite prepared to find that it is only distantly related to religion. This very announcement of subjects, with fetching and surprising titles, marks a departure from the usage of the past and reveals another idea of the place of the Bible. And the situation is now so common that it may be useful to face this question: Should the preacher in ordinary circumstances confine himself to the Bible, or, in other words, should religion alone be his subject?

It goes without saying that of all public men to him belongs the liberty of speech, and speech has been the most powerful instrument in forming character and making history. Brave and honest words have been more potent than the sword or all the treasures of gold. Those sounds which pierce the ear and those black marks upon the page have broken the fetters of tyranny and beaten down unrighteousness and inspired with hope despairing humanity and opened the vision of heaven amid the clouds of this earthly travail. "Those poor bits of rag-paper with black ink on them," says Carlyle, "from the daily newspaper to the sacred Hebrew Book! For indeed whatever be the outer form of the thing (bits of paper as we say and black ink) is it not verily at bottom the highest act of men's faculties that produces a book?" But the spoken word will ever be more effectual than the written—not only because it is plainer but because it is stronger. From the pulpit of St. Gile's in Edinburgh Knox reigned as a king over Scotland, although he was often a lonely and forsaken man. His sermons had such power that Randolph, the English Ambassador, wrote to Cecil, "Where your honour exhorteth us to stoutness I assure you the voice of one man is able to put more life in us than fyve hundreth trumpettes continually blustering in our ears." The real maker of life is the speaker and therefore on him lies a heavier responsibility to do his work with a good conscience and with all his might. The prophet who betrays his trust is the chief traitor of the race. And therefore the minister must be very careful of his commission both as to what its contents are and how he is to discharge it.

Every one who has anything true to tell—whether he be a man of letters like Carlyle or a man of science like Darwin—is in his measure a prophet, but the minister of Christ is the prophet in excelsis, and this because of the gravity and dignity of his message. He has not received a roving commission to wander up and down the Universe of Knowledge. His subject is fixed, but its definition is not a limitation, it is rather a concentration. As Christ's representative he must take his latitude from his Master, and Christ concerned Himself alone with the relation of the human soul to God and all that is contained in that fellowship. Whether in the Temple or on the hillside, whether discoursing in the synagogue or conversing with His disciples along the sweet country ways, Jesus was ever speaking of His Heavenly Father, of the foolish prodigal in the far country, of the degradation of sin, of the engaging beauty of holiness, of the wholesome discipline of the cross, and the comfortable hope of our Father's House. Jesus insisted from first to last on religion, and ought not Religion to be the lifelong text of the Christian minister's sermons? Here is a message which must be forever fresh because contemporaneous with every generation, a message which must be ever in demand because it is an answer to the hunger of the human soul.

One is not amazed that a preacher of the lower and coarser order, a man without intellectual or spiritual culture, without vision or ideals, should reduce the pulpit to a raree-show and meet the competition of a gutter press with a gutter pulpit. But one is astounded when some able and earnest man turns aside from that Evangel which is the heart and glory of the Bible to descant upon poets and novelists, upon makers of philosophy and leaders of the democracy, upon the problems of politics and the laws of commerce, upon the achievements or the crimes of the day. One pities the preacher who has so despaired of the Bible that he depends for a message upon the last distinguished name in the obituary or the last flaming sensation of the week, and is empty-handed if Saturday comes without a death or a scandal. Browning, it is true, always remains a last resource and Mazzini has for certain minds a mysterious fascination which never fails, but there cannot be an earthquake every week or a first-class social scandal. The nervous system of this kind of modern preacher must be severely tried. It is one thing to have the mine of the Bible rich and inexhaustible for your working, and another to go out prospecting through the wilderness of the press for an attractive subject. Passing by the anxious uncertainty of the preacher to the times, who knows not whether there may be anything found for Sunday wherewith to tickle the ears of the groundling, there are various serious reasons against this non-Biblical and secular style of preaching.

The first which occurs to one's mind is that it has no authority behind it. When one notices that a certain school of preachers include within their range science, literature, the drama and politics, to say nothing of stranger subjects, and that the only things which are ostracized are the necessities, the aspirations, the trials and the hopes of the human soul in her highest and most religious mood, then he is tempted to be critical. What is this man thinking of who will deliver himself on anything however tedious or unpleasant but will have nothing to do with the Evangel? By whom was he called to his life-work? For what was he trained at his college? What office does he hold in the eyes of the world? Is it not in virtue of being a servant of Christ that he stands in that pulpit? Has his whole education not been to fit him for the exposition of the Bible? Has he not been raised above the crowd of men and given his vantage ground upon the foundation of the Christian Church? And does the historic Church of Christ exist to furnish a half-educated public with literary institute lecturers or flaming journalists, and is her message to the world a piquant review of the week's news? If one feels that this semi-literary, semi-social *causerie* be his proper calling in life, let him hire a room and deliver it to any audience who may care to listen, but he has no moral right to employ the Christian pulpit for this trifling end. Who ordained him to teach English Literature or Natural Science, and does he really suppose that he can deal with those subjects better than an expert? Will not this man be twice discredited, first because he has travelled into another province than his own, and secondly, because he is a stranger in it? He has obtained the most imposing and influential position in the world on false pretenses; he has frivolously perverted the most august commission given to any human being.

It may also be fairly pointed out that this rechauffe of stale news or this second rate review of current literature is not what people are expecting from the pulpit or what they come to hear. He is really a simple minded person who believes that a congregation gathers to hear him discourse on the details of their own business—that the politicians are hungering for more politics, and the merchants for commerce and the scholars for a new translation of the classics and the scientist for the latest discovery in radium. Human nature is so constituted that every man, weary with his six days professional work, desires an escape and a change—to find relief in another world from that which for the time has grown to him familiar and stale. Hearers not only long for something new; they are secretly hoping for a lift. After six days commonplace they cry for inspiration, for a glimpse through the gates into the City of Gold, for a break in the gray clouds above their heads. When we take for granted, as we are apt to do, that the average man who talks with you about the weather and the price of produce is indifferent to the spiritual and wearies of its exposition, we do him less than justice and forget that men are reticent about their souls; no one can imagine how sincerely and wistfully this matter of fact, prosaic, and if you like, worldly man, is hoping to hear a word which will quicken and straighten him for the week's work. If he gets what he wants, this hearer may never thank the preacher in an effusive letter because he is shy about such matters and has not the gift of religious expression, but he will come again to the same preacher; if he be disappointed he will not complain but he will have one reason less for going to church. And it will not matter how clever and up-to-date and common sense and secular the sermon was; if it had no word for the soul, this tired, world-worn, half-sceptical man will have no use for it. He can get this arid, unspiritual stuff anywhere, from an evening paper or in the Exchange; he wanted something from above. Is it not cruel to disappoint that thirsty man? Is it not an irony that a modern preacher will imagine that he is pleasing this man of the world with the chatter of the clubs and the market place, when he is dumbly waiting for the Kingdom of God? Must not this preacher incur a double condemnation because he received a message and refused to deliver it, and because men reasonably expected that message at his hand and did not obtain it? There are many lecture rooms where intelligent people can study Wordsworth and Darwin; many meetings where citizens can hear about education and sanitation; but there is only one Christian pulpit where immortal beings can be warned against their sins and comforted in their sorrows, where peace can be proclaimed by the Cross of Christ and the struggling, disheartened soul confirmed in the hope of everlasting life. If the pulpit fail in its own high function, of which indeed it has the monopoly, then all the journalists and lecturers, all the teachers of science and literature in the land united together, cannot repair the loss or take the empty place. The minister of Christ had better settle with his conscience where he is to put his strength —whether he is to be general dealer, supplying more or less acute and useful criticism on a hundred present day questions, or an ambassador of Christ discharging with all his might the duties of his commission. It is good that he should be, if possible, a man of letters, to appreciate the construction of the Bible, and a student of philosophy to grasp the principles of religion; it is good that he be in touch with the life of the world to apply the medicine to its wounds, and that he be a public-spirited citizen to sanctify the commonwealth by the spirit of Jesus. But his first concern and his imperative charge is the eternal welfare of the human soul.

Perhaps, however, it may be urged that this is falling back on the belated standpoint of our fathers and limiting the true humanity of the public. Is not this also sinking below the comprehensiveness of the Bible to which nothing human is alien? Will not the modern say that in preaching on Art and Politics and Books and Sociology the Christian minister is carrying out the spirit of the Incarnation and sanctifying the remotest provinces of human thought and activity? Can we not find Religion in every department of knowledge, and identify the Christ in the most unexpected circumstances? This line of argument is very specious but it rests on a confusion of thought about the order and method of Christianity. According to Jesus the Kingdom of God was not a state regulat-

THE USE OF THE BOOK

ing all the affairs of human life, it was a condition of soul. The Kingdom of God was within a man, and Jesus dealt in the first instance not with the commonwealth but with the individual. The supreme effort of our religion is not to reform society in bulk but to regenerate its members one by one. A man renewed in mind and heart, in conscience and will is its ideal. Then the new man will make a new state as the influence passes from the centre to the circumference. Christianity did not begin by lecturing on the classics or art, it made its appeal to the soul, and offered a means of deliverance from sin and a way of access unto God. Upon this line Christianity succeeded and upon the same line it has always been most effectual. But the leaven hid in human nature worked till the whole was leavened. If a man's nature is quickened and inhabited by the Spirit of Christ it will flower in all directions. He will begin to think ; he will grow enterprising, he will rebel against bondage, he will acquire a sense of beauty, he will come to be in love with knowledge. Christianity in the mouths of the Apostles was an Evangel and it will ever remain the message of God to men. But Christianity has created the modern University; it has been the mother of modern music, painting, sculpture and letters—Raphael and Dante, Michael Angelo, and Bacon had been impossible without Christianity; it has founded the Western civilization and is the guardian of Justice; it has been the spring of freedom, and to-day national and municipal order in the West rest on the principles of our religion. Mr. Cotter Morison who was a trenchant critic of Christianity points out in his "Service of Man," "The intellectual revival which followed the spread of Christianity and gave to the world the whole literature of the fathers, Greek and Latin, in the third, fourth and fifth centuries at the very time when Pagan literature had fallen into sterility and decrepitude, . . . of all writers who have used Latin as their mother tongue it is no exaggeration to say that St. Augustine is the most original, suggestive and profound. He is a genuine thinker, not a mere rhetorician like Cicero, Seneca and the rest." And he goes on to say, "The controversies of the fourth century which have given rise to much tasteless ridicule, notably the Arian controversy and the witticism suggested that it was preposterous that the world should be divided into hostile camps by a diphthong, these controversies were mentally the most stimulating discussions, not only which the age admitted of but which had ever occupied men's minds, . . . the difference between 'homoousion' and 'homoiousion' is only that of a single letter, but as Emile Saisset well said, 'Probe the matter to the bottom; between Jesus Christ, man, and Jesus Christ, man-God, there is infinity; there is, if one may so speak, the whole thickness of Christianity.'" If Christianity be an Evangel it has been also a culture and a civilization. It has been the maker of men and therefore of society.

With the Bible as his text-book the preacher has a wide range of subjects and it may be useful to review the chief kinds of preaching, noting both their strength and their weakness. The study of character has very rich material in Holy Scripture and there is no type which has not its vivid and convincing illustration. The usefulness of such studies is that they fling both virtues and vices into bold relief, the one for imitation and the other for avoidance, and that hearers are unconsciously led to love the good and to hate the evil. They are drawn to St. John and repelled from Judas Iscariot as it were automatically. For this style of preaching one needs practical knowlege of life, insight into motive, appreciation of evidence and a genuine dramatic instinct. Two minds of quite opposite class will never succeed with character sermons—that which delights itself in subtle analysis and psychological classification because this is for philosophy and not for popular instruction, and the other which is at home with the doctrine and ill at ease with a living person. It is the shrewd, observant, genial, sympathetic mind, which is most successful with character, and gathers the most practical lessons of daily life. The wise minister, even though he may have the gift of portraiture will use it with a measure of reserve since the mass of the people, while vastly enjoying an occasional likeness either of saint or sinner will soon begin to miss the aid and stimulus of practical exhortation. The spiritual life cannot be maintained on character studies, any more than the mind on fiction.

As so much space is given in the Old Testament to history and the revelation of God is made through its medium, it is desirable that a congregation should know the broad outlines of the Hebrew annals and that their wealth of incident should be laid under contribution for didactic purposes. People should not be bored with ancient genealogies and lists of empty names, or with minute geographical details and sketches of distant and unimportant battlefields. But the struggles of the Judges for national existence, the creation of the Jewish kingdom, the causes which led to its disruption, the character of Solomon's court, the influence of foreign civilization, the relations of the Jewish State to neighbouring nations, the internal friction between rich and poor, and the tragedy of the exile, all these are of lasting interest not only because the situations formed links in the development of that life which was crowned with the coming of the Messiah, but because they are repeated, circumstances being changed, in every national history. While it is not expedient that the preacher should teach politics and while it were madness of him to venture into party conflict he ought to make politicians in his church, men of wisdom who understand the signs of the times, men of God who will do righteousness, and he can attain this end by extracting from the crises of Jewish history those principles of government which save and glorify a nation. From this ancient story one gathers, without straining any point or playing tricks with what may be called meta-politics, those laws of mercy and righteousness which run in all lands and in all ages, and by which alone the commonwealth can prosper. By the works of God in the former days, His chastisements and His deliverances, a nation may be taught to depart from foolishness and to follow after godliness. Thoughtful people will be vastly interested and instructed by historical sermons, but although of great value as character studies, they should not be allowed to usurp too large a place in the proportion of a man's preaching. Preachers must not forget that as they discourse on this heroic scale, dealing with kings and nations, there may be many in the congregation so crushed by family sorrow and so perplexed by personal duty that they cannot follow those large themes, and will require homelier food than this feast of magnificence.

3 A third and more practical form of Bible teaching is ethical, and no student of Holy Scripture can complain that in our day more stress is laid on the moral than on the theological side of religion. It is a distinct gain that preachers can deal boldly with the duty and necessity of good works without being accused of denying the gospel and that the most insidious and dangerous of all heresies— Rabbi Duncan, the Scotch Hebrew scholar,

used to say it was the only one—Antinomianism, is almost dead. With psalms like the fifteenth and the twenty-fourth, with passages like the first and fifty-eighth chapters of Isaiah, with the Sermon on the Mount and the Epistle of St. James, the preacher has a strong message to deliver on godly living, and should lift up his voice like a trumpet against the shortcomings and inconsistencies of professing Christians. Hypocrites should be pilloried without mercy, for Jesus showed none to the Scribes and Pharisees, and cant should be scourged in the pulpit with fierier zeal and more utter contempt than in the press, for the Church has suffered more by tricky and dishonourable Christians than by all the attacks of her critics from Celsus to Voltaire. The time has come for declaring that the capitalist who treats his workmen unjustly, but gives large subscriptions to foreign missions, or the merchant who makes a shameful bankruptcy but takes part in religious meetings, can no more be tolerated in Christian society, and that he only can be regarded as an honest and orthodox Christian who keeps Christ's law and sets an example of brave living. One of the most clamant subjects for careful and thorough treatment is Bible ethics, and one longs for more books like that admirable treatment by Dr. Newman Smyth. The Church must give its special attention to one province where a keen attack is being made on morals, and that is the family. Both in fiction and in the drama, as well as in certain socialistic quarters, the sanctity and authority of the marriage bond are being ridiculed and condemned. Upon the Church of Christ lies the burden of the defense, and once more she may prove herself the saviour of society. The deliverance of women from slavery and their elevation to a just place beside men, the establishment of monogamy and the protection of the child, are among the most beneficent achievements of Christianity. What has been won must not be lost, and it is one of the duties laid upon the pulpit in our time to protest against the growing fashion of divorce and to safeguard on every side the holy estate of matrimony. Upon the pure and united family as on a sure foundation rests both Church and State, and the day marriage is superseded or slighted by vagrant love the dissolution of society will begin. If, however, ethics are to be a living practice and not a doctrinal theory, they must be related to faith and made the fruitage of the Christ life. The eleventh and twelfth chapters of the Epistle to the Romans must not be separated. Upon the doctrine of salvation which St. Paul celebrates in the Doxology at the close of his doctrinal arguments, "Oh, the depth of the riches both of the wisdom and the knowledge of God, . . . for of Him and through Him and to Him are all things, to whom be glory forever and ever. Amen," is grounded his irresistible appeal for noble living. "I beseech you therefore, brethren, by the mercies of God that ye present your bodies a living sacrifice, holy, acceptable to God, which is your reasonable service." This is the Bible idea of ethics, the fulfillment and the revelation of the Christ life.

There are two kinds of preaching which

have fallen out of fashion in late days, and might be revived with considerable benefit to congregations; one is what used to be called experimental. By this is meant the treatment of the intimate commerce between the soul and God, and on this pious people of the past laid great stress. Preachers of a spiritual cast of mind dealt at length and often most ingeniously with the phases of faith, the changing temperature of the affections towards God, the varying moods of despair, hope, penitence, joy, with backsliding and restoration, with the hiding of God's face, and dryness in prayer, with the languishing of the graces and their reinforcement, with the secret fellowship in the sacrament and the heavenly rapture when a saint beholds his Lord face to face. Those were the themes of the mediæval mystics and the finest Roman saints. They are treated at length by men so different as Rutherford, the Scots theologian, and Faber the hymn writer, but they used to be the almost daily theme of ordinary ministers up and down the land. They spoke to the people of things which were real because people were then exercised in the affairs of the soul. The eye was turned inward and earnest Christians gave themselves to introspection. Meditation was not yet a lost art like the making of Venetian glass, but was practiced by all who were following the religious life. The soul was ever being examined, its ways explored, and its habits described, and an expert in the lore of the soul was highly esteemed. The preacher who could explain the symptoms of spiritual health and disease was ranked higher than the most eloquent teacher of duty or even than the expounder of doctrine. Humble and unlettered people could write a commentary on Psalms like the twenty-second, " My God, my God, why hast Thou forsaken me"; or the fortieth, " I waited patiently for the Lord; and He inclined unto me and heard my cry; " or the forty-second, " Why art thou cast down oh, my soul, and why art thou disquieted in me. Hope thou in God for I shall yet praise Him who is the help of my countenance and my God;"or the Fifty-first Psalm, " Cast me not away from Thy presence nor

THE USE OF THE BOOK

take Thy Holy Spirit from me;" or the one hundred and thirtieth, "Out of the depths have I cried unto Thee, O Lord." They were human documents in those days, not mere pieces of stately phrase; they were the intimate journal of the soul. This delicate and spiritual teaching has now become an antiquarian curiosity or is regarded as an admirable fact of higher life conferences. Whether our religion be exoteric or not it is no longer esoteric; if the stream of religion run broadly and cover a large expanse, it has ceased to run strongly and to cut a deep channel. Piety talks so much now that it has not time to think; it is so busy with charitable works that it has no place for spiritual research. The kingdom of God is not now within a man—a presence of the Eternal in the soul; it is scattered abroad through society, committees, a babel of talk and endless conferences. One fears that under the spirit of restless activity religion has lost its reverence and peace, its penitence and humility, its fragrance and tenderness. Is it not time that we were entering into our chamber and closing the door; that we were learning to be quiet and to wait on God; that preachers after exhausting themselves on every kind of enterprise should turn their attention to the life of the soul. If the scientist will spend a year upon the construction and habits of a worm, the teacher of religion may spend many years upon the natural history of the soul. It would come as a surprise upon many congregations if their minister should turn from the health of the city and the question of amusements and the analysis of the last popular book and the morals of an election campaign and speak to his people of their own complex spiritual nature with its unexpressed feelings, its haunting fears, its amazing visions, its unsuspected dangers. Until religion be rooted in experience it can never be either sure or rich, and it still remains true that though we have the Bible in our hands and worship for our aid, it is within the soul each man must meet with God. The drawback to experimental preaching now as in the past—and against this we must be on our guard—is that it is apt to make religion too

THE USE OF THE BOOK

subjective, and to build faith rather upon the moods of the individual than upon the Word of God. It almost came to this, with certain skilled masters of experience; not he that believeth but he that feeleth is saved; they insisted so much on the varieties of faith, on the changing dispositions of the mind, on the degree of grace, on the exercises of piety. Good people were inclined to pull out their faith to see if it were growing, and to be ever testing their love to see if it were real, till they lived between extremes of the highest joy or the darkest despair, according as the clouds revealed or hid the sun. They were apt to forget that the clouds rolled from their own nature as from a marshy plain, and that the sun was eternal in the heavens; that their salvation did not depend on their changing moods but on the Unchanging Love of God. Ebenezer Erskine, the eminent Scots minister, during his last illness was visited by a relative who came to see him and began to comfort him thus—" I hope you get now and then a blink to bear up your spirit under your affliction." Erskine answered with much sense and courage, "I know more of words than of blinks. Though He slay me yet will I trust in Him. The covenant is my charter, and if it had not been for that blessed word my hope and strength had perished from the Lord." And Dr. Chalmers, another of the worthies of the Kirk, exhorted a sick person who was looking too much within and too little towards Christ with convincing force, "I beseech you do not cast your anchor within the hold of the ship." We know too little of ourselves to-day, and a return to a wise measure of experimental preaching is distinctly required. But salvation stands forever in the knowledge of God, and while our moods are like the shifting ocean He is the Rock which abideth.

Another style of preaching, which is now rarely heard, is exposition, by which is meant taking a book of the Bible and opening up its meaning verse by verse from beginning to end. Expository preaching reached its height in Scotland in the eighteenth century when preachers continued upon one text for a month and would preach upon the

Epistle to the Romans for a generation. There was something amiss when from childhood to middle age the people of a parish were imprisoned in one Epistle, and one can understand the feeling of the worthy hearer who declared himself worn out by those Ephesians. The method was to occupy the former half of every sermon with a review of the sermon preceding and then to take up the following verse. Partly owing to the tediousness of this preaching, partly owing to new forms such as the character study and the ethical discourse which came into fashion last century, congregations now rarely hear a book of Scripture expounded in order, and this is a loss both to the preacher and the hearer. For one thing, expository preaching secures that large and connected portions of the Bible shall be presented to the minds of the people, and not merely perpetually varying and disconnected texts. In the course of exposition a preacher is able also to touch in passing upon many practical subjects which would hardly warrant a full discourse and which perhaps indeed he would have some delicacy in taking up unless they came in the regular way of his exposition. There are crises in a man's ministry when he is haunted with the idea that he has finally delivered his message and that his preaching material is exhausted. He feels himself growing stale and unprofitable; he is afraid that he can no longer lead the flock into new and green pastures. It would be a departure for a minister in those circumstances to take a book of the Bible or a subject stretching through several books and make it the subject of careful and detailed exposition. Professor A. B. Bruce, who was one of the strongest men in the Scotch Church of our time and one of the most suggestive writers, tells us how he came to write what is perhaps his best book, "The Training of the Twelve." "During an autumnal holiday I was in such a distempered condition of body that all thoughts and feelings were dead and I dreaded the prospect of returning to pastoral duty, being sensible of mental vacuity. At length my perplexities shaped themselves into a prayer that I might

THE USE OF THE BOOK

be led into green pastures as the old ones were all nibbled bare. Shortly after my thoughts reverted to the lesson given to the Catechumen's Class (Notes of Sermons on Christ's intercourse with the Twelve Disciples) and I at once resolved to make these the subject of a course of lectures." Professor Bruce says his studies proved to be green pastures to himself at least. And certainly they have been rich feeding ground for Christian ministers. "The Training of the Twelve" is not only one of the weightiest volumes in the department of pastoral theology but it is also a suggestive model of the new form of expository preaching. Modern congregations would not endure the verse to verse commentary, and there is not one man in a thousand who could make this minute textual exposition either intelligible or useful. What is needed is, either that the preacher take some large subject and then pursue it, say, through the Prophets or the Gospels or the Psalms or the Epistles, as the case may be, setting it in the light of the Book which he is using, and so expounding ideas rather than words; or, if one book is taken, to fasten upon its half dozen leading themes and set them forth in order without going into every hole and corner of the book, and without pretending to open up the meaning of every word. It appears to me that this style of preaching in the hands of a man who has a scholarly knowledge of the Bible and a comprehensive mind, which will not be mastered by details, but make details serve him, would build up a congregation in faith and knowledge. For the success of this preaching it is necessary that the course of sermons on any book be limited in number, and that the preacher through patient study have a firm and confident hold of his subject.

No review of preaching, especially preaching based on the Bible, would be complete without a reference to the evangelistic sermon. As the Bible is an appeal of God to the human soul and especially an appeal to those who have gone into the far country, it surely lies upon every minister of the Evangel to address himself from time to time to those who are outside faith and strangers to Christ. The evangelistic sermon has suffered reproach partly because it has not as a rule been prepared with sufficient care and partly because it has been too frequently repeated. There is an unhappy contrast made between other sermons, theological, ethical, or historical, and the evangelistic sermon or address as it is often called. While the former are expected to be more or less elaborate, the latter is described with the idea of compliment as simple. While the phrase "The simple Gospel" sounds well, it has done much injury because it is really a depreciation of the message of the Bible and a sanction for shallow and ineffectual speech. In one sense the gospel is simple as great works of art, poems or pictures, are "*simplex munditiis*" but this does not mean that the gospel is slight or silly. It is not by sentimentality or by twaddle, it is not with the repetition of conventional phrases or a multitude of words without ideas that the preacher can win either prodigals or unbelievers to the faith and obedience of his Master. It is only by the most sympathetic study of their needs, by the most vigorous reasoning regarding the problems of religion, by the most gracious presentation of the Person of Christ and by the loftiest treatment of the ideals of life that alien minds can be conciliated and those that are afar off be brought near. Above all things worn out catch-words must be thrown aside and conventional arguments be replaced by fresh statements of the truth. It is said that a worthy but commonplace evangelist was once offering a prayer before his address which ran largely upon these lines—"Lord, give us power. We want power. We want much power. We want power to-day. We want power now. We want power for the old. We want power for the young. . . ." So he would have gone on for ten minutes simply because he did not know what to say next, and could only repeat himself, had not a voice called out from the meeting, "It isn't power you want, it's ideas." It was a rude and irreverent interruption but it touched his weakness as with the point of a needle. What is wanted in

THE USE OF THE BOOK

most evangelistic sermons is strong thinking and worthy style; the Evangelist requires to be a hard student of Bible Truth and a diligent reader of English Classics. From the proportions of truth in the Bible and from our knowledge of the human mind the minister will learn that the evangelistic address should only come at wide intervals since nothing is more destructive than for a congregation to become gospel-hardened and to grow accustomed to the chief appeal which can be made to the human soul. The Evangel should come as a surprise and a new message, with the dew of the morning upon it.

Two kinds of preaching I submit may be omitted without loss; and one is the critical sermon. No question troubles a young minister entering upon his work more than this. Ought I to give my people the results of Bible criticism; and, if I am going to do so, what is the most expedient plan? If I do not say anything then I shall be suspected of dishonesty and practicing the doctrine of reserve; besides in that case they will learn from other lips what is being done and their faith may be upset. On the other hand, the critical treatment of the Bible in the pulpit may offend many members of my congregation and may be very uninteresting to others. Ministers must be guided by the circumstances of their work, but, speaking generally, it seems out of keeping with the spirit of the Bible itself to occupy the too short time given to the minister for his sermon with what is literary information. As Ruskin says, the preacher "has but thirty minutes to get at the separate hearts of a thousand men, to convince them of all their weaknesses, to shame them for all their sins, to warn them of all their dangers, to try by this way and that to stir the hard fastenings of those doors where the Master Himself has stood and knocked and yet none opened, and to call at the openings of those dark streets where Wisdom herself has stretched forth her hands and no man regarded; thirty minutes to raise the dead in." Surely it were a pity to take up the thirty minutes with a discussion of the documents which go to

THE USE OF THE BOOK

form the Pentateuch or to enter into the question of the two Isaiahs. The minister who will stop to peddle with questions of authorship and date in the course of his gospel exposition is a pedant and ought to be behind the lecture desk and not in the Christian pulpit. The large principles of Bible construction such as we have been discussing ought to be assumed and if criticism throws a direct pencil of light upon any separate Scripture it ought to be used, but the detailed results of criticism should not be brought into the pulpit but be taught in a Bible Class.

The other form of ineffectual and really foolish preaching occupies itself with the trifles of Bible History or its obsolete incidents. Within the last few years I heard with mine own ears an earnest and able minister spend a considerable part of his sermon upon the badger-skins of the Tabernacle, explaining that they were got not from a badger but from some other kind of beast, I do not remember what, and that they symbolized a certain doctrine I do not know what, but as I looked round a large country congregation I wondered why their excellent minister had not found somewhere in the length and breadth of Holy Scripture a more timely and practical subject. The Tabernacle indeed seems to cast a less than happy fascination over many minds, for one of the most saintly ministers in Scotland used to lecture upon it in classes year after year, and used to reconstruct it by a working model, and, although he was the most reverent of men, he would at a certain stage strike a match and place the light inside the little contrivance to show the glory of God in the Holiest of All. It may be a matter of taste, but personally I am more interested in the fact (although I have never used it in pulpit exposition) that when the prodigal was received with music, the word shows that the instrument was what we would call the bagpipe. I think that I could make as much out of those bagpipes welcoming the prodigal as out of the badger-skins of the Tabernacle, but as time is short and the Bible has many majestic themes, I suggest that no minister should waste even one Sunday upon the curiosities of its texts or history.

For indeed, and this would be my last word, the supreme end of preaching is one which lifts a man above antiquarian investigations and historical disquisitions, for he is set with every power that is in him, with all his knowledge, his passions, his pity, his humanity, to reconcile man to God. It is the preacher's duty to expound the moral law written on the Tables of Stone and also on the fleshy tables of our hearts, to lift up his voice against the madness of sin, and to remind his hearers of its just punishment; and he will judge it wise to bring his people from time to time under the awful shadow of Mount Sinai, but this is only a stage on the journey, and he will fail in his charge if he does not land his hearers at Mount Calvary, for his commission is not one of judgment but of mercy. Again, it is his duty from time to time to assemble his hearers on that Mountain of Galilee where Jesus laid down the New Law of the Kingdom; but he will not be content till he has brought them to that "Green Hill, Far Away" where Christ by His Passion and Sacrifice broke the bonds of sin and opened the fountain of the new obedience unto all believers, for he is not merely the preacher of duty, he is the preacher of grace. His work, according to the spirit of the Bible, is to lay hold of his fellow men in their exile and to persuade them to return unto their Father, and once he has induced them to set their faces homeward never to let them go till they have arrived. The dark disaster of human life is the quarrel of the soul with God. We are not at home with God, and we are therefore ill at ease. We have an evil conscience, we are discontented with circumstances, we carry a rebellious will, within us is an aching heart. It is the business of philosophers to make their peace with law. It is the business of religion to invite men to make their peace with God, who is behind all law, and it is the high privilege of God's ambassador to declare that on God's side peace is made and a welcome is waiting. Christ by His Perfect Obedience in life and death, by His Sacrifice on Calvary, and

His Resurrection from the dead, by His Ascension into heaven and His Eternal Intercession, has made an open way from the furthest country of sin and shame into which the most foolish soul has wandered to the Home and to the Heart of God. There is no barrier in this way and no one to forbid the returning sinner. The wayfaring man though he be a fool shall not err therein and the blind shall be led by a way that they know not. And to make the highway of life more easy and alluring it has been strown from the beginning to the end thereof with invitations and promises, with entreaties and assurances. Along it the angels of grace are ever travelling to guide the weary, wayworn wanderers home, and among those angels I dare to include the preacher of the Evangel. Is any office so inspiring as his, any work so charged with blessing? It is his to heal the bitterest controversies of human life, and to make the most lasting peace; at the same moment to fill with gladness the heart both of God and man; by the same service to deliver him who was ready to perish and to minister unto Christ of the travail of his soul. For his word every man is waiting within the heart, for the sound of his feet every one must have a welcome. "How beautiful upon the mountains are the feet of Him that bringeth good tidings, that publisheth peace, that bringeth good tidings of good, that publisheth salvation."

References.

Geo. Adam Smith — The Prophets. 3/.
Prof Ramsay — Acts of Apostles 3/
Prof Moulton — Literary Study of Bible 4/
Matt. Arnold — Literature + Dogma
God + the Bible

Dr. Newman Smyth.
Prof. A. B. Bruce — Training of the Twelve.